celebrating
QUICK BREADS
AND PASTRIES

Orange-Pumpkin Muffins
and Oatmeal Muffins,
recipes on page 57

LEISURE ARTS, INC.
Little Rock, Arkansas

Library of Congress Control Number: 2010942050
ISBN-13: 978-1-60900-116-2

contents

Sugarplum Tarts,
recipe on page 128

Banana-Crunch Loaves,
recipe on page 27

celebrating
QUICK BREADS
AND PASTRIES

Whether for snacking or to complement a meal, quick breads and pastries are delicious family favorites! No one can resist the aroma of fresh-baked Brownie Nut Bread or the temptation of Cranberry-Apple Turnovers with luscious fruit filling peeking out. This mouth-watering collection from the Leisure Arts Test Kitchen presents 75 sweet and savory quick breads, biscuits, muffins, turnovers, tarts, breakfast rolls, and other pastries. Every recipe is shown in up-close, full-color photography, with a complete ingredients list and clear directions. To further ensure your success, we've included baking advice from the experts and general kitchen tips. Enjoy!

Bacon Batter Bread (top)
and Swiss Cheese Bread,
recipes on page 32

SUCCESS WITH BREADS

You can be most successful at baking quick breads and pastries when you know a few tips from the pros. Here are some of our favorites.

BAKING TIPS

- Make sure to use fresh baking powder, baking soda, and self-rising flour.
- Preheat your oven long enough for it to reach the correct temperature given in the recipe.
- For convenience and efficiency, organize all your ingredients and tools before you start mixing or cooking.
- For flaky doughs, keep butter cold until you are ready to cut it into the dry ingredients.
- For lighter and fluffier breads and biscuits, don't overmix the dough.
- When rolling pie crust, sprinkle the work surface and the dough frequently (but sparingly) with flour to prevent sticking and to minimize absorption of the extra flour into the dough, which would make it tougher.
- When you need to drizzle a small amount of icing or topping and you do not have a pastry bag, use a resealable plastic bag. After filling bag half full of icing or topping, seal the bag and cut off a small tip of one corner. Make your first snip small, as you can always cut off more if needed.
- Bake one loaf or pan of the recipe at a time on the center rack of a preheated oven. If baking two loaves or pans at a time, space evenly for good air circulation.
- Oven temperatures vary, so always check your bread or pastry 1 minute before the earliest time stated in recipe, to prevent overbaking.

SUPPLIES

- Many cooks prefer clear glass pans for pies and other pastry because of how efficiently glass conducts heat and because you can see when the bottom crust is sufficiently browned.
- Use heavy-gauge, shiny aluminum bread pans. Dark coating on pans will affect browning.
- Use sharp, thin biscuit cutters and press straight down (and remove straight up). Twisting the cutter prevents biscuits from rising as high.

STORAGE TIPS

- After completely cooling bread, store each kind separately in an airtight container to prevent flavors from blending. Use waxed paper between loaves or muffins to prevent them from sticking together.
- Store crisp breads or pastries in a tin or container with a loose-fitting lid. In humid areas, the lid will need to be tighter.
- Fruit pastries may be kept at room temperature for one day. Cream-filled pastries or those with cheese or meat must be refrigerated with air-tight wrapping.
- Most breads can be frozen up to six months. Freeze in plastic freezer bags or plastic containers with tight-fitting lids.

GIFT PRESENTATION IDEAS

- Homemade breads make wonderful gifts! To present your baked goods in style, try some of the gift-wrapping and presentation ideas on page 141.

QUICK BREADS

Why do we call them quick breads? You guessed it—you can mix them up quickly and bake on a whim, without kneading endlessly and waiting hours for them to rise. Our recipes provide a delicious sampling of the variations that are possible!

A quick bread with a cake-like texture, this delightful treat features crushed pineapple, chopped dates, and crunchy walnuts.

pineapple-date-nut bread

Line two $8^1/_2$ x $4^1/_2$-inch loaf pans* with waxed paper and grease waxed paper. Set pans aside.

In a large bowl, combine flour, sugar, baking powder, baking soda, and salt. In a small bowl, beat together buttermilk, oil, egg, and vanilla. Stir undrained pineapple into buttermilk mixture. Make a well in center of dry ingredients; stir in liquid ingredients just until blended. Stir in dates and walnuts. Spoon batter into prepared pans.

Bake in a preheated 350° oven for 45 to 55 minutes or until a toothpick inserted in center of bread comes out clean and top is lightly browned. Cool in pans 10 minutes. Remove from pans and serve warm or cool completely on a wire rack.

YIELD: 2 loaves

***NOTE:** Our bread was baked in two 7 x 4-inch oven-safe paper-lined wooden baskets.

- 3 cups all-purpose flour
- $^3/_4$ cup sugar
- $1^1/_2$ teaspoons baking powder
- $^1/_2$ teaspoon baking soda
- $^1/_2$ teaspoon salt
- $^3/_4$ cup buttermilk
- $^1/_3$ cup vegetable oil
- 1 egg
- 1 teaspoon vanilla extract
- 1 can (8 ounces) crushed pineapple
- 1 cup chopped dates
- 1 cup chopped walnuts

Here's a delicious recipe you can use all through the year. This moist bread calls for canned cranberry sauce and either fresh or frozen blueberries.

cranberry-blueberry bread

Grease a 9 x 5-inch loaf pan; set aside.

In a medium bowl, combine flour, baking soda, baking powder, and salt. In a large mixing bowl, cream sugar and butter. Beat in eggs and buttermilk. Stir in dry ingredients, blending well. Stir in cranberry sauce and blueberries. Pour batter into prepared pan.

Bake in a preheated 375° oven for 1 hour and 10 minutes or until a toothpick inserted in center of bread comes out clean. Remove from pan and cool on a wire rack.

YIELD: 1 loaf

3	cups all-purpose flour
1	teaspoon baking soda
1	teaspoon baking powder
1	teaspoon salt
1	cup sugar
½	cup butter or margarine, softened
2	eggs
1	cup buttermilk
1	cup whole-berry cranberry sauce
1	cup fresh or frozen blueberries, thawed if frozen

Starting with brownie mix and biscuit mix, Brownie-Nut Bread (bottom, in photo) offers homemade taste without all the work. Creamy Cinnamon Spread helps to bring out the rich flavor. Pineapple-Pumpkin Bread (top) is equally easy, based on pound cake mix.

pineapple-pumpkin bread

Line bottoms of two 8$\frac{1}{2}$ x 4$\frac{1}{2}$-inch loaf pans wih waxed paper. Grease and flour waxed paper and sides of pans. Set pans aside.

In a large bowl, combine cake mix, pumpkin pie spice, and baking soda. Add pumpkin, undrained pineapple, and eggs; beat until well blended. Stir in pecans. Spoon batter into prepared pans.

Bake in a preheated 325° oven for 45 to 55 minutes or until a toothpick inserted in center of bread comes out clean. Cool in pans 20 minutes. Remove from pans and serve warm or cool completely on a wire rack.

YIELD: 2 loaves

- 1 package (16 ounces) pound cake mix
- 2 teaspoons pumpkin pie spice
- 1 teaspoon baking soda
- 1 cup canned pumpkin
- 1 can (8 ounces) crushed pineapple
- 2 eggs
- 1 cup chopped pecans

brownie-nut bread

Lightly grease 2 nonstick 8$\frac{1}{2}$ x 4$\frac{1}{2}$-inch loaf pans;* set aside.

In a medium bowl, beat brownie mix, buttermilk biscuit mix, water, eggs, oil, and vanilla with an electric mixer until well blended. Stir in chocolate chips, pecans, and raisins until well blended. Pour batter into prepared pans.

Bake in a preheated 350° oven for 45 to 50 minutes or until a toothpick inserted near center of bread comes out with a few crumbs clinging to it. Cool in pans on a wire rack 10 minutes. Run a knife around edges of pans to loosen bread; remove from pans. Cool on wire rack 10 minutes longer. Serve warm with Creamy Cinnamon Spread.

YIELD: 2 loaves

*****NOTE:** Our bread was baked in six 4 x 2$\frac{1}{2}$-inch pans for 30 to 35 minutes.

For Creamy Cinnamon Spread, beat cream cheese, confectioners sugar, cinnamon, and vanilla in a small bowl until well blended. Store in an airtight container in refrigerator. Serve at room temperature.

YIELD: about 1 cup spread

- 1 package (21.5 ounces) brownie mix
- 1 package (5.5 ounces) buttermilk biscuit mix
- $\frac{2}{3}$ cup water
- 2 eggs
- $\frac{1}{4}$ cup vegetable oil
- 1 teaspoon vanilla extract
- 1 package (6 ounces) semisweet chocolate chips
- 1 cup chopped pecans
- $\frac{1}{2}$ cup raisins

CREAMY CINNAMON SPREAD

- 1 package (8 ounces) cream cheese, softened
- 3 tablespoons confectioners sugar
- 1 teaspoon ground cinnamon
- $\frac{1}{2}$ teaspoon vanilla extract

Inspired by Amish friendship bread, this dense delight relies on buttermilk to provide its rich taste without the on-going care and feeding of a starter batter. The versatile recipe is great for experimenting with different pudding flavors, spices, nuts, and other add-ins.

pudding bread

Grease two 8¹/₂ x 4¹/₂-inch loaf pans* and coat with sugar; set aside.

In a large bowl, combine pudding mixes and buttermilk. Stir in oil, 1 cup sugar, eggs, apple pie spice, vanilla, baking powder, salt, and baking soda; stir until well blended. Gradually stir in flour and then pecans. Pour batter into prepared pans. Combine cinnamon and remaining 2 tablespoons sugar; sprinkle mixture on top of batter.

Bake in a preheated 325° oven for 1 hour or until a toothpick inserted in center of bread comes out clean. Cool in pans 10 minutes. Remove from pans and cool completely on a wire rack.

YIELD: 2 loaves

***NOTE:** Our bread was baked in a 9 x 5-inch ceramic loaf pan for 1 hour and 30 minutes.

1 package (5.1 ounces) vanilla instant pudding mix
¹/₂ package (3.4 ounces) pistachio instant pudding mix
1 cup buttermilk
1 cup vegetable oil
1 cup plus 2 tablespoons sugar, divided
3 eggs
2 teaspoons apple pie spice
1 teaspoon vanilla extract
1¹/₂ teaspoons baking powder
¹/₂ teaspoon salt
¹/₂ teaspoon baking soda
2¹/₂ cups all-purpose flour
1¹/₄ cups chopped pecans
¹/₄ teaspoon ground cinnamon

This delicious bread gets a surprising start with crushed graham crackers. Then it's mixed with chopped pecans and shredded carrots. Drizzled icing makes it oh-so appetizing!

cinnamon-carrot bread

For bread, grease two 8$\frac{1}{2}$ x 4$\frac{1}{2}$-inch loaf pans. Line bottoms of pans with waxed paper; grease waxed paper. Set pans aside.

In a medium bowl, combine cracker crumbs and pecans; set aside. In a large bowl, combine sugar, oil, eggs, and orange extract; beat until blended. Stir in carrots. In a small bowl, combine flour, cinnamon, salt, and baking powder. Add flour mixture to oil mixture; stir just until moistened. Spoon half of batter into prepared pans. Sprinkle about 6 tablespoons crumb mixture over batter in each pan; swirl mixture with a knife. Spoon remaining batter over crumb mixture. Sprinkle remaining crumb mixture on top.

Bake in a preheated 350° oven for 38 to 43 minutes or until a toothpick inserted in center of bread comes out clean and top is golden brown. Cool in pans 10 minutes. Remove from pans and cool completely on a wire rack.

For icing, combine confectioners sugar, water, and orange extract in a small bowl; stir until smooth. Drizzle icing over bread. Allow icing to harden.

YIELD: 2 loaves

BREAD

- $\frac{3}{4}$ cup coarsely crushed cinnamon graham crackers (about five 2$\frac{1}{2}$ x 5-inch crackers)
- $\frac{3}{4}$ cup chopped pecans
- 1 cup sugar
- $\frac{3}{4}$ cup vegetable oil
- 2 eggs
- $\frac{1}{2}$ teaspoon orange extract
- 1 cup shredded carrots
- 1$\frac{1}{3}$ cups all-purpose flour
- 1 teaspoon ground cinnamon
- $\frac{1}{2}$ teaspoon salt
- $\frac{1}{2}$ teaspoon baking powder

ICING

- $\frac{3}{4}$ cup confectioners sugar
- 1 tablespoon water
- $\frac{1}{2}$ teaspoon orange extract

Packed with garden-fresh zucchini, this wholesome bread is a palate pleaser. Bake it in pint canning jars to create pretty serving shapes or for convenient gift-giving.

zucchini-bran bread

Grease and flour 5 pint-size wide-mouth canning jars; set aside.

In a large bowl, beat eggs and oil until foamy. Add zucchini, sugar, and vanilla, mixing well. In a small bowl, combine flour, cereal, cinnamon, baking soda, salt, and baking powder. Add flour mixture to zucchini mixture, stirring just until combined. Stir in walnuts.

Spoon batter into prepared jars, filling each jar just over half full. Place jars on a baking sheet and bake in a preheated 325° oven for 40 to 45 minutes or until a toothpick inserted in center of bread comes out clean. Place jars on a wire rack to cool.*

Bread may also be baked in two 8$\frac{1}{2}$ x 4$\frac{1}{2}$-inch loaf pans for 50 to 60 minutes in a preheated 350° oven.

YIELD: 5 jars or 2 loaves

***NOTE:** This is not a canning technique; bread should be eaten fresh or stored in the refrigerator or freezer.

3   eggs
1   cup vegetable oil
2   cups shredded zucchini
2   cups sugar
1   tablespoon vanilla extract
2   cups all-purpose flour
1   cup whole bran cereal
1   tablespoon ground cinnamon
1   teaspoon baking soda
$\frac{1}{2}$ teaspoon salt
$\frac{1}{4}$ teaspoon baking powder
1   cup chopped walnuts

Flavored gelatin gives luscious color to easy Strawberry Bread (top, in photo), made with biscuit mix and frozen fruit. Not overly sweet, the old-fashioned Short'nin' Bread is the perfect complement to fresh strawberries or the fruit of your choice.

strawberry bread

Grease and flour two $8^1/_2$ x $4^1/_2$-inch loaf pans; set aside.

In a large bowl, combine biscuit mix, sugar, gelatin, and lemon peel. Reserving $1/_2$ cup strawberry juice ($^3/_4$ cup strawberry juice, if using glaze*), drain strawberries. Reserving remaining strawberries if making glaze, add 1 cup strawberries, $1/_2$ cup reserved strawberry juice, and eggs to dry ingredients. Beat at low speed of an electric mixer 30 seconds; increase to high speed and beat 3 minutes longer. Spoon batter into prepared pans.

Bake in a preheated 350° oven for 40 to 50 minutes or until a toothpick inserted in center of bread comes out clean. Cool in pans 10 minutes. Remove from pans and cool on a wire rack (with waxed paper underneath if using glaze).

If glaze is desired, combine 1 cup confectioners sugar, $^1/_4$ cup reserved strawberry juice, and remaining reserved strawberries in a small bowl; beat until smooth. Drizzle glaze over warm bread. Allow glaze to harden.

YIELD: 2 loaves

*NOTE: Our bread was not glazed.

3 cups buttermilk biscuit mix

$1/_2$ cup sugar

1 package (3 ounces) strawberry-flavored gelatin

1 teaspoon dried lemon peel

1 carton (24 ounces) frozen sweetened sliced strawberries, thawed and divided

3 eggs

OPTIONAL: 1 cup confectioners sugar for glaze

short'nin' bread

Lightly grease a baking sheet; set aside.

In a large bowl, combine flour, sugar, baking powder, and salt. Using a pastry blender or two knives, cut shortening into dry ingredients until mixture resembles coarse meal. In a small bowl, beat egg and milk together. Pour egg mixture into flour mixture and stir until thoroughly moistened. Drop about $1/_3$ cupful of dough into mounds on prepared baking sheet.

Bake in a preheated 450° oven for 12 to 15 minutes or until lightly browned. Remove from baking sheet and cool on a wire rack. Serve with fresh strawberries and whipping cream.

YIELD: about 8 shortcakes

2 cups all-purpose flour

$^1/_4$ cup sugar

1 tablespoon baking powder

$^3/_4$ teaspoon salt

$1/_2$ cup vegetable shortening

1 egg

$1/_2$ cup milk

Fresh strawberries and whipping cream to serve

Canned peaches and pears transform these two recipes into fabulous favorites. We used petite loaf pans for our Pear Bread (bottom, in photo), but if you adjust the baking time you could use standard loaf pans, as we did for the Cinnamon-Peach Bread.

cinnamon-peach bread

Line the bottoms of two 8$\frac{1}{2}$ x 4$\frac{1}{2}$-inch loaf pans with waxed paper; grease pans and waxed paper. Set pans aside.

In a large bowl, combine flour, sugars, cinnamon, mace, baking soda, and salt. In a medium bowl, beat peaches, eggs, and oil with an electric mixer until well blended. Add peach mixture to dry ingredients; stir until well blended. Spoon batter into prepared pans.

Bake in a preheated 350° oven for 50 to 60 minutes or until a toothpick inserted in center of bread comes out clean. Cool in pans 10 minutes. Remove from pans and serve warm or cool completely on a wire rack.

YIELD: 2 loaves

3	cups all-purpose flour
1$\frac{1}{2}$	cups granulated sugar
$\frac{1}{2}$	cup firmly packed brown sugar
1$\frac{1}{2}$	teaspoons ground cinnamon
$\frac{1}{4}$	teaspoon ground mace
1	teaspoon baking soda
1	teaspoon salt
1	can (15$\frac{1}{4}$ ounces) peach slices in heavy syrup, drained
4	eggs
1	cup vegetable oil

pear bread

Grease and flour four 5$\frac{1}{2}$ x 3-inch loaf pans; set aside.

Reserving $\frac{1}{4}$ cup pear juice, drain pears and coarsely chop. In a large bowl, sift together flour, sugar, salt, and baking soda. Add reserved pear juice, eggs, and oil to dry ingredients; beat until smooth. Stir in pears and walnuts. Pour batter into prepared pans.

Bake in a preheated 350° oven for 30 to 35 minutes or until a toothpick inserted in center of bread comes out clean. Cool in pans 10 minutes. Remove from pans and serve warm or cool completely on a wire rack.

YIELD: 4 loaves

1	can (29 ounces) pear halves
2	cups all-purpose flour
1	cup sugar
1	teaspoon salt
1	teaspoon baking soda
2	eggs
$\frac{1}{2}$	cup vegetable oil
$\frac{1}{2}$	cup chopped walnuts

Fresh cranberries add color and tart flavor to this spicy sweet bread, which is chock full of tender apples and chunky pecans.

apple-cranberry-nut bread

Line the bottom of a 9 x 5-inch loaf pan with waxed paper; grease pan and waxed paper. Set pan aside.

Process apple pieces and cranberries in a food processor until coarsely chopped. In a large bowl, combine flour, sugar, baking powder, baking soda, salt, and apple pie spice. In a small bowl, combine orange juice, oil, egg, orange zest, and vanilla. Stir orange juice mixture, apple mixture, and pecans into dry ingredients just until blended. Spoon batter into prepared pan.

Bake in a preheated 350° oven for 55 to 60 minutes or until a toothpick inserted in center of bread comes out clean and top is golden brown. Cool in pan 10 minutes. Remove from pan and cool completely on a wire rack.

YIELD: 1 loaf

1 medium baking apple, peeled, cored, and cut into pieces (about 1$\frac{1}{2}$ cups)

1 cup fresh cranberries

2 cups all-purpose flour

1 cup sugar

2 teaspoons baking powder

$\frac{1}{2}$ teaspoon baking soda

$\frac{1}{2}$ teaspoon salt

$\frac{1}{2}$ teaspoon apple pie spice

$\frac{1}{2}$ cup orange juice

$\frac{1}{4}$ cup vegetable oil

1 egg

1 teaspoon grated orange zest

1 teaspoon vanilla extract

1 cup chopped pecans

As this moist banana bread bakes, its candied pecan topping develops an irresistible crunch. Sharing is easy when you make it in petite loaves like these.

banana-crunch loaves

Grease eight $5^3/_4$ x 3-inch loaf pans; set aside.

For candied pecan topping, beat egg whites in a medium bowl until soft peaks form. In a small bowl, combine brown sugar, cinnamon, vanilla, and salt; beat into egg whites. Fold in pecans; set aside.

For bread, cream butter, shortening, and sugar in a large bowl until fluffy. Add eggs and egg yolks, 1 at a time, beating well after each addition. Beat in bananas and vanilla.

In a medium bowl, combine flour, baking powder, and baking soda. Alternately beat dry ingredients and buttermilk into batter, beating until well blended. Spoon batter into prepared pans. Spoon pecan topping over batter.

Bake in a preheated 325° oven for 50 to 60 minutes or until a toothpick inserted in center of bread comes out clean. Cool in pans 10 minutes. Remove from pans and cool completely on a wire rack.

YIELD: 8 loaves

CANDIED PECAN TOPPING

- 2 egg whites
- $^1/_2$ cup firmly packed brown sugar
- 1 teaspoon ground cinnamon
- 1 teaspoon vanilla extract
- $^1/_8$ teaspoon salt
- 3 cups chopped pecans

BREAD

- $^1/_2$ cup butter or margarine, softened
- $^1/_2$ cup shortening
- $2^3/_4$ cups sugar
- 4 eggs
- 2 egg yolks
- $1^1/_4$ cups mashed bananas (about 3 medium bananas)
- $1^1/_2$ teaspoons vanilla extract
- 3 cups all-purpose flour
- $^1/_4$ teaspoon baking powder
- $^1/_4$ teaspoon baking soda
- 1 cup buttermilk

A traditional favorite, spicy gingerbread gets extra flavor from strongly brewed coffee, golden raisins, and grated orange zest.

golden raisin gingerbread

Line the bottom of a 9 x 5-inch loaf pan with waxed paper; grease pan and waxed paper. Set pan aside.

In a large bowl, cream butter and brown sugar until fluffy. Add eggs and molasses; beat until smooth. In a small bowl, combine flour, cinnamon, baking powder, baking soda, and cloves. Alternately add dry ingredients and coffee to creamed mixture; stir until well blended. Stir in raisins, ginger, and orange zest. Pour batter into prepared pan.

Bake in a preheated 350° oven for 45 for 55 minutes or until a toothpick inserted in center of bread has a few crumbs clinging and top is golden brown. Cool in pan 10 minutes. Remove from pan and serve warm or cool completely on a wire rack.

YIELD: 1 loaf

- $1/2$ cup butter or margarine, softened
- $1/2$ cup firmly packed brown sugar
- 2 eggs
- $1/2$ cup molasses
- 2 cups all-purpose flour
- 1 teaspoon ground cinnamon
- $3/4$ teaspoon baking powder
- $1/2$ teaspoon baking soda
- $1/4$ teaspoon ground cloves
- $1/2$ cup hot strongly brewed coffee
- $1/3$ cup golden raisins
- $1/4$ cup finely chopped crystallized ginger
- 1 tablespoon grated orange zest

Perfect for holiday gift-giving and entertaining, this flavorful sweet bread improves with age and keeps well for up to three months. It's a beautiful blend of fresh cranberries, zesty orange peel, chopped pecans, and a medley of spices.

cranberry keeping bread

Grease and flour two 8$\frac{1}{2}$ x 4$\frac{1}{2}$-inch loaf pans;* set aside.

In a large saucepan, combine 1$\frac{1}{2}$ cups cranberries, sugar, and orange zest. Bring to a boil and cook, stirring constantly, until berries pop and mixture thickens (about 5 minutes). Remove from heat. Chop remaining cranberries and add to the cranberry mixture; cool.

In a large bowl, combine flour, brown sugar, cinnamon, nutmeg, allspice, cloves, baking soda, and salt. In a small bowl, beat eggs with sour cream. Stir egg mixture into dry ingredients. Stir in butter, cranberry mixture, and pecans. Pour batter into prepared pans and bake in a preheated 350° oven for 1 hour or until a toothpick inserted in center of bread comes out clean.

Cool bread in pans 10 minutes. Remove from pans and cool completely on wire racks. Wrap bread in aluminum foil and allow to age 1 week. The flavor will continue to improve over several weeks. The bread will keep for up to 3 months in a cool, dry place.

YIELD: 2 loaves

NOTE: Our bread was baked in three 6 x 3-inch oven-safe cardboard containers at 350° for 45 to 50 minutes.

3	cups fresh cranberries, divided
$\frac{3}{4}$	cup granulated sugar
$\frac{1}{2}$	teaspoon grated orange zest
2$\frac{1}{4}$	cups all-purpose flour
2	cups firmly packed brown sugar
2	teaspoons ground cinnamon
$\frac{1}{2}$	teaspoon ground nutmeg
$\frac{1}{2}$	teaspoon ground allspice
$\frac{1}{4}$	teaspoon ground cloves
2	teaspoons baking soda
1	teaspoon salt
2	eggs
$\frac{3}{4}$	cup sour cream
$\frac{1}{2}$	cup butter or margarine, melted
1	cup coarsely chopped pecans

Hearty texture brings mouth-watering good looks to these two tasty breads. Bacon Batter Bread (top, in photo) is brimming with smoky flavor, while the mini loaves of Swiss Cheese Bread are ultra mellow with a hint of dill.

bacon batter bread

Grease a 9 x 5-inch loaf pan;* set aside.

In a large skillet, cook bacon over medium heat until crisp. Transfer to paper towels to drain; reserve $1/3$ cup bacon drippings. Cool bacon to room temperature, crumble, and set aside.

In a large bowl, combine flour, sugar, baking powder, and salt. In a medium bowl, whisk together reserved bacon drippings, milk, eggs, and smoke flavoring. Add egg mixture to dry ingredients; stir just until moistened. Fold in bacon. Pour batter into prepared pan.

Bake in a preheated 350° oven for 45 to 50 minutes or until a toothpick inserted in center of bread comes out clean. Cool in pan 10 minutes. Remove from pan and cool completely on a wire rack.

YIELD: 1 loaf

***NOTE:** Our bread was baked for 30 to 35 minutes in two $8^1/_2$ x $4^1/_2$-inch loaf pans that were lined with paper liners.

- 1 pound bacon
- 3 cups all-purpose flour
- $1/4$ cup sugar
- 2 tablespoons baking powder
- 2 teaspoons salt
- $1^1/_2$ cups milk
- 3 eggs
- $1/2$ teaspoon liquid smoke flavoring

swiss cheese bread

Grease seven $5^1/_2$ x 3-inch loaf pans;* set aside.

In a large bowl, combine flour, sugar, baking powder, and salt. Using a pastry blender or 2 knives, cut butter into dry ingredients until mixture resembles coarse meal. Stir in cheese and dill weed. In a medium bowl, whisk together milk and eggs. Add milk mixture to flour mixture; stir just until moistened. Pour batter evenly into prepared pans.

Bake in a preheated 400° oven for 20 to 25 minutes or until a toothpick inserted in center of bread comes out clean. Cool in pans 10 minutes. Remove from pans and serve warm or cool completely on a wire rack.

YIELD: 7 mini loaves

***NOTE:** Our bread was baked for 13 to 15 minutes in eight 4 x $2^1/_2$-inch greased ceramic loaf pans.

- 4 cups all-purpose flour
- 2 tablespoons sugar
- 1 tablespoon baking powder
- $1^1/_2$ teaspoons salt
- $1/2$ cup butter or margarine, chilled and cut into pieces
- 4 cups (16 ounces) shredded Swiss cheese
- 1 tablespoon dried dill weed
- 2 cups milk
- 2 eggs

Cheesy Pepper Bread (shown in pan) gets its richness from cream cheese and its zippy taste from Monterey Jack cheese with jalapeño peppers. Quick Dill Bread is a flavorful loaf seasoned with dill seed and dried minced onion.

cheesy pepper bread

Line a 9 x 5-inch loaf pan with wax paper; grease paper and set aside.

In a medium bowl, combine cream cheese and butter; beat until fluffy. Add eggs and milk; beat until well blended. Beat in cheese, pimiento, and onion. In a large bowl, combine flour, baking powder, salt, and pepper. Add cream cheese mixture; stir just until blended. Spoon into prepared pan.

Bake in a preheated 350° oven for 50 to 55 minutes or until golden brown. Cool in pan 5 minutes. Remove from pan; serve warm or cool completely on a wire rack and serve toasted.

YIELD: 1 loaf

1	package (8 ounces) cream cheese, softened
2	tablespoons butter or margarine, softened
2	eggs
1/2	cup milk
1 1/2	cups shredded Monterey Jack cheese with jalapeño peppers
1	jar (2 ounces) chopped pimiento, drained
1	tablespoon chopped green onion
2	cups all-purpose flour
2	teaspoons baking powder
1/4	teaspoon salt
1/8	teaspoon ground black pepper

quick dill bread

Grease two 7 1/2 x 3 1/2-inch loaf pans and line with waxed paper; set aside.

In a medium bowl, combine flour, sugar, and baking powder. Using a pastry blender or 2 knives, cut in butter until mixture resembles coarse meal. In a small bowl, whisk milk, eggs, dill seed, and minced onion until well blended. Add to flour mixture; stir just until moistened. Spoon batter into prepared pans.

Bake in a preheated 350° oven for 35 to 45 minutes or until bread is golden brown and a toothpick inserted in center of bread comes out clean.

Cool bread in pans on a wire rack 10 minutes. Remove from pans and serve warm or cool completely on a wire rack.

YIELD: 2 loaves

3	cups all-purpose flour
1/2	cup plus 2 tablespoons sugar
1 1/2	tablespoons baking powder
2/3	cup butter or margarine
1	cup milk
4	eggs
5	teaspoons dill seed
2	teaspoons dried minced onion

A unique combination of sweet potatoes and yellow cornmeal, these lightly sweetened and spiced corn sticks are delicious served warm with butter.

sweet potato corn sticks

Brush a 7-mold corn stick cast-iron pan generously with vegetable oil; heat in oven 10 minutes.

In a large bowl, combine sweet potatoes, buttermilk, butter, and eggs, mixing until smooth. In a separate bowl, combine cornmeal, flour, sugar, baking powder, cinnamon, allspice, and salt. Add to sweet potato mixture, stirring just until combined. Spoon batter into prepared pan, filling each mold about two-thirds full.

Bake in a preheated 400° oven for 15 to 20 minutes or until browned around the edges. Serve warm.

YIELD: about $2^1/_2$ dozen corn sticks

$1^1/_2$ cups cooked, peeled, and mashed sweet potatoes (about 2 medium potatoes)

$^1/_2$ cup buttermilk

$^1/_3$ cup butter or margarine, melted

2 eggs

1 cup yellow cornmeal

1 cup all-purpose flour

$^1/_3$ cup sugar

$2^1/_2$ teaspoons baking powder

1 teaspoon ground cinnamon

$^1/_2$ teaspoon ground allspice

$^1/_2$ teaspoon salt

This zesty alternative to ordinary cornbread is sure to be a welcome surprise at the dinner table. Cream-style corn, Cheddar cheese, and crumbled bacon pack it with amazing flavor.

super mexican cornbread

Grease 4^1/$_2$-inch-wide star-shaped baking pans or muffin cups; set aside.

In a medium bowl, combine flour, cornmeal, baking powder, sugar, salt, and baking soda. Stir in buttermilk, cheese, corn, oil, eggs, peppers, and bacon. Spoon batter into prepared pans, filling each pan about two-thirds full.

Bake in a preheated 375° oven for 25 to 30 minutes or until a toothpick inserted in center of cornbread comes out clean. Serve warm.

YIELD: about 8 cornbread stars or 15 muffins

1 cup all-purpose flour

^{3}/$_4$ cup yellow cornmeal

1^1/$_2$ teaspoons baking powder

1 teaspoon sugar

1 teaspoon salt

^{1}/$_2$ teaspoon baking soda

1 cup buttermilk

1 cup (4 ounces) shredded sharp Cheddar cheese

1 can (8^1/$_2$ ounces) cream-style corn

^{1}/$_4$ cup vegetable oil

2 eggs, beaten

2 tablespoons seeded and chopped jalapeño peppers

6 slices bacon, cooked and crumbled

Tempt hearty appetites with tasty Southwest Olive Bread. No one will ever guess how easy it was to prepare using cornmeal mix and stuffed olives. This fast-and-easy recipe will fit right into your busy schedule.

southwest olive bread

Grease and flour four $5^1/_2$ x 3-inch loaf pans; set aside.

In a medium bowl, combine cornmeal mix, cumin, and red pepper. Add milk, eggs, and oil; stir until well blended. Add cheese and olives, stirring well. Spoon batter into prepared pans.

Bake in a preheated 375° oven for 35 to 40 minutes or until bread is golden brown and a toothpick inserted in center of bread comes out clean. Cool in pans on a wire rack 5 minutes. Run a knife around edges of pans to loosen bread; remove from pans. Serve warm.

YIELD: 4 loaves

3 cups self-rising yellow cornmeal mix

1 teaspoon ground cumin

$^1/_4$ teaspoon ground red pepper

$1^1/_2$ cups milk

2 eggs

$^1/_4$ cup vegetable oil

1 cup (4 ounces) shredded sharp Cheddar cheese

1 jar (10 ounces) whole stuffed green olives, drained

MUFFINS

It's no wonder muffins are such a mainstay in the baking world. Most require the simplest of ingredients and only a minimum of preparation. Best of all, their individual serving sizes let you grab one and go on with your busy life. How sweet!

Pretty paper liners make each of these Almond Muffins a party in itself. Chopped almonds in the batter and sprinkled on top add nutty taste and crunchy texture.

almond muffins

Line muffin pan with paper baking cups; set aside.

In a medium bowl, combine flour, brown sugar, baking powder, baking soda, and salt. Stir in 1 cup almonds. In a small bowl, combine buttermilk, melted butter, eggs, and extracts. Make a well in center of dry ingredients and add buttermilk mixture; stir just until moistened. Spoon batter into prepared pan, filling each cup about one-half full. Sprinkle remaining 2 tablespoons almonds over batter.

Bake in a preheated 350° oven for 20 to 25 minutes or until lightly browned and a toothpick inserted in center of muffin comes out clean. Remove from pan; serve warm or cool on a wire rack.

YIELD: about 1 dozen muffins

$1^1/_3$ cups all-purpose flour

$^1/_2$ cup firmly packed brown sugar

1 teaspoon baking powder

$^1/_2$ teaspoon baking soda

$^1/_4$ teaspoon salt

1 cup plus 2 tablespoons chopped sliced almonds, toasted and divided

$^1/_2$ cup buttermilk

$^1/_4$ cup butter or margarine, melted

2 eggs, beaten

$^1/_2$ teaspoon vanilla extract

$^1/_2$ teaspoon almond extract

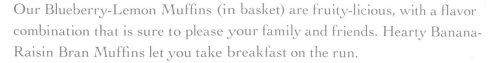

Our Blueberry-Lemon Muffins (in basket) are fruity-licious, with a flavor combination that is sure to please your family and friends. Hearty Banana-Raisin Bran Muffins let you take breakfast on the run.

blueberry-lemon muffins

Lightly grease cups in a muffin pan; set aside.

Combine flour, baking powder, sugar, and salt in a medium bowl. Combine milk, butter, egg, and vanilla in a small bowl. Add milk mixture to dry ingredients; stir just until moistened. Stir in lemon zest and blueberries. Spoon batter into prepared pan, filling each cup about three-fourths full.

Bake in a preheated 450° oven for 20 minutes or until lightly browned and a toothpick inserted in center of muffin comes out clean. Remove from pan; serve warm or cool on a wire rack.

YIELD: about 1 dozen muffins

- 2 cups all-purpose flour
- 1 tablespoon baking powder
- 3/4 cup sugar
- 1/2 teaspoon salt
- 1 cup milk
- 1/4 cup butter or margarine, melted
- 1 egg, lightly beaten
- 1 teaspoon vanilla extract
- 1 1/2 cups blueberries, fresh or frozen, rinsed
- 1 1/2 teaspoons grated lemon zest

banana-raisin bran muffins

Line muffin pans with paper baking cups; set aside.

In a medium bowl, combine flours, sugar, baking powder, baking soda, and salt. In a small bowl, whisk together eggs, buttermilk, oil, and bananas. Add buttermilk mixture and raisin bran flakes to dry ingredients; stir just until moistened. Spoon batter into prepared pans, filling each cup about two-thirds full.

Bake in a preheated 350° oven for 25 to 30 minutes or until lightly browned and a toothpick inserted in center of muffin comes out clean. Remove from pan; serve warm or cool on a wire rack.

YIELD: about 1 1/2 dozen muffins

- 1 cup all-purpose flour
- 3/4 cup whole-wheat flour
- 1/3 cup sugar
- 2 teaspoons baking powder
- 1/2 teaspoon baking soda
- 1/2 teaspoon salt
- 2 eggs
- 1/2 cup buttermilk
- 1/2 cup vegetable oil
- 2 medium bananas, mashed
- 2 cups raisin bran flakes

If you want the family to stick around for breakfast, set out a basket of Cinnamon Puffins hot from the oven. These tender treats smell so-oooo good, dipped in butter and coated with cinnamon-sugar right before serving!

cinnamon puffins

Lightly grease muffin pan; set aside.

In a medium bowl, combine flour, baking powder, $1/2$ teaspoon nutmeg, and salt. In another medium bowl, beat $1/2$ cup sugar, shortening, egg, and vanilla until well blended. Add dry ingredients to creamed mixture; beat in milk until smooth. Spoon batter into prepared pan, filling each cup about two-thirds full.

Bake in a preheated 350° oven for 20 minutes or until lightly browned and a toothpick inserted in center of puffin comes out clean. Melt butter in a small saucepan. In a small bowl, combine remaining $1/2$ cup sugar, cinnamon, and remaining $1/2$ teaspoon nutmeg. Dip warm puffins in butter, then in sugar mixture, coating thoroughly. Serve warm.

YIELD: about 1 dozen puffins

$1^{1}/_{2}$	cups all-purpose flour
$1^{1}/_{2}$	teaspoons baking powder
1	teaspoon ground nutmeg, divided
$1/2$	teaspoon salt
1	cup sugar, divided
$1/3$	cup shortening
1	egg
$1/2$	teaspoon vanilla extract
$1/2$	cup milk
$1/2$	cup butter or margarine
1	teaspoon ground cinnamon

With or without flamboyant paper baking cups, these spicy Apple Cake Muffins will earn raves for their good looks and great taste. They're made with Granny Smith apples, a world favorite for their crisp, tart taste and beautiful green color.

apple cake muffins

Line muffin pans with paper baking cups;* set aside.

In a medium bowl, stir together flour, baking powder, $1/2$ teaspoon cinnamon, salt, allspice, and nutmeg. In a large bowl, cream butter and $3/4$ cup sugar until fluffy. Add eggs, oil, and vanilla; stir until smooth. Add dry ingredients to creamed mixture; stir until well blended. Finely chop reserved apple peel. Stir in apples, apple peel, and walnuts. Spoon batter into prepared pans, filling each cup about three-fourths full.

Bake in a preheated 400° oven for 15 to 18 minutes or until a toothpick inserted in center of muffin comes out clean. Remove from pans; transfer muffins to a wire rack.

In a small bowl, stir together remaining 2 tablespoons sugar and $1/8$ teaspoon cinnamon. Sprinkle tops of warm muffins with sugar mixture; serve warm or cool on a wire rack.

YIELD: about $1^{1}/2$ dozen muffins

***NOTE:** Our muffins were baked in nine $3^3/4$-inch high tulip-shaped brown paper baking cups.

$2^1/4$	cups all-purpose flour
$3/4$	teaspoon baking powder
$1/2$	teaspoon plus $1/8$ teaspoon ground cinnamon, divided
$1/4$	teaspoon salt
$1/4$	teaspoon ground allspice
$1/4$	teaspoon ground nutmeg
$1/4$	cup butter or margarine, softened
$3/4$	cup plus 2 tablespoons sugar, divided
3	eggs
$1/2$	cup vegetable oil
1	tablespoon vanilla extract
2	cups peeled, cored, and chopped Granny Smith apples, reserving peel from 1 apple
$1/2$	cup chopped walnuts

Cheery cherries are always good for a smile! These miniature muffins, filled with bits of maraschino cherries and chopped almonds, are ready to pop in your mouth for pure delight.

mini cherry muffins

Line miniature muffin pans with paper baking cups; set aside.

Reserving $1/4$ cup cherry juice, drain and coarsely chop cherries. In a large bowl, combine flour, sugar, baking powder, lemon zest, and salt. In a small bowl, whisk together reserved cherry juice, milk, oil, egg, and almond extract. Make a well in center of dry ingredients and add milk mixture; stir just until moistened. Stir in cherries and almonds. Spoon batter into prepared pans, filling each cup about three-fourths full.

Bake in a preheated 400° oven for 14 to 17 minutes or until lightly browned and a toothpick inserted in center of muffin comes out clean. Remove from pans; serve warm or cool on a wire rack.

YIELD: about 2 dozen mini muffins

- 1 jar (10 ounces) maraschino cherries
- 1³/4 cups all-purpose flour
- ³/4 cup sugar
- 2 teaspoons baking powder
- 1¹/2 teaspoons grated lemon zest
- ¹/2 teaspoon salt
- ¹/2 cup milk
- ¹/3 cup vegetable oil
- 1 egg
- 1 teaspoon almond extract
- ¹/4 cup chopped slivered almonds

These plump golden muffins are bursting with goodness! Enriched with sour cream, the moist blend of dried cranberries and toasted pecan pieces bakes up looking terrific with a generous sprinkling of sugar.

cranberry-pecan muffins

Line muffin pan with paper baking cups; set aside.

In a medium bowl, combine flour, 1 cup sugar, baking soda, and salt. Using a pastry blender, cut butter into dry ingredients until mixture resembles coarse meal. Stir in sour cream, cranberries, pecans, and orange zest. Spoon batter into prepared pan, filling each cup about two-thirds full. Sprinkle with remaining 6 tablespoons sugar.

Bake in a preheated 400° oven for 18 to 20 minutes or until lightly browned and a toothpick inserted in center of muffin comes out clean. Remove from pan; serve warm or cool on a wire rack.

YIELD: about 1 dozen muffins

2	cups all-purpose flour
1	cup plus 6 tablespoons sugar, divided
1	teaspoon baking soda
1/2	teaspoon salt
1/2	cup chilled butter, cut into pieces
2	cups sour cream
1	cup sweetened dried cranberries, chopped
1/2	cup chopped pecans, toasted
1 1/2	teaspoons grated orange zest

Nutty Sweet Potato Muffins are a great start for the day, but they're also a delicious choice to pack in a sack lunch or to enjoy as an afternoon snack. They make a tasty comeback for leftover sweet potatoes, or you can use canned ones.

nutty sweet potato muffins

Line muffin pans with paper baking cups; set aside.

For topping, combine brown sugar, flour, pecans, oil, and cinnamon in a small bowl until well blended; set aside.

For muffins, combine flour, cinnamon, baking soda, allspice, and salt in a medium bowl. In another medium bowl, beat sweet potatoes, sugar, oil, eggs, and vanilla. Add dry ingredients to sweet potato mixture; beat until well blended. Stir in pecans. Spoon batter into prepared pans, filling each cup about two-thirds full. Sprinkle about $1^{1}/_{2}$ tablespoons topping over batter in each cup.

Bake in a preheated 350° oven for 20 to 25 minutes or until a toothpick inserted in center of muffin comes out clean. Cool in pans 5 minutes. Remove from pans; serve warm or cool on a wire rack.

YIELD: about 16 muffins

TOPPING

$^{1}/_{2}$ cup firmly packed brown sugar

$^{1}/_{2}$ cup all-purpose flour

$^{1}/_{2}$ cup chopped pecans

3 tablespoons vegetable oil

$^{1}/_{2}$ teaspoon ground cinnamon

MUFFINS

$2^{1}/_{4}$ cups all-purpose flour

$1^{1}/_{2}$ teaspoons ground cinnamon

1 teaspoon baking soda

$^{1}/_{2}$ teaspoon ground allspice

$^{1}/_{2}$ teaspoon salt

1 cup cooked and mashed sweet potatoes (or canned sweet potatoes, drained and mashed)

1 cup sugar

$^{1}/_{2}$ cup vegetable oil

2 eggs

$^{1}/_{2}$ teaspoon vanilla extract

$^{1}/_{2}$ cup chopped pecans

Topped with a generous sprinkling of chopped walnuts, Orange-Pumpkin Muffins beckon to be devoured. Moist Oatmeal Muffins are naturally delicious.

orange-pumpkin muffins

Line muffin pans with paper baking cups; set aside.

In a small bowl, combine flour, pumpkin pie spice, baking soda, baking powder, and salt. In a large bowl, combine sugars, eggs, and oil. Add pumpkin, orange juice, and orange zest to sugar mixture; beat until well blended. Stir in dry ingredients just until blended. Spoon batter into prepared pans, filling each cup about two-thirds full. Sprinkle about 1 teaspoon walnuts over batter in each cup.

Bake in a preheated 350° oven for 20 to 23 minutes or until a toothpick inserted in center of muffin comes out clean. Remove from pans; serve warm or cool on a wire rack.

YIELD: about 1¹/₂ dozen muffins

1³/₄	cups all-purpose flour
1¹/₂	teaspoons pumpkin pie spice
1	teaspoon baking soda
¹/₂	teaspoon baking powder
¹/₂	teaspoon salt
1	cup granulated sugar
¹/₂	cup firmly packed brown sugar
2	eggs
¹/₃	cup vegetable oil
1	cup canned pumpkin
¹/₃	cup orange juice
1	teaspoon grated orange zest
¹/₂	cup chopped walnuts

oatmeal muffins

Lightly grease muffin pan; set aside.

Process oats in a food processor until coarsely ground. Add flours, sugar, baking powder, baking soda, and salt to food processor; pulse process just until well blended. In a medium bowl, beat buttermilk, oil, and eggs until well blended. Add dry ingredients to buttermilk mixture; stir just until moistened. Spoon batter into prepared pan, filling each cup about two-thirds full.

Bake in a preheated 400° oven for 15 to 18 minutes or until a toothpick inserted in center of muffin comes out clean. Remove from pan; serve warm or cool on a wire rack.

YIELD: about 1 dozen muffins

1	cup old-fashioned oats
¹/₂	cup all-purpose flour
¹/₄	cup whole-wheat flour
¹/₂	cup sugar
2	teaspoons baking powder
¹/₂	teaspoon baking soda
¹/₂	teaspoon salt
¹/₂	cup buttermilk
¹/₃	cup vegetable oil
2	eggs

With one simple recipe, you can make all these tasty variations: Basic Muffins (from left), Cream Cheese, Mocha-Nut, Cornmeal-Cheese, and Oatmeal.

tasty muffins

Make the basic muffin recipe or one or more of the variations.

Lightly grease miniature muffin pans; set aside.

In a medium bowl, combine flour and sugar. Make a well in center of dry ingredients. In a small bowl, combine milk, melted butter and eggs; beat until well blended. Pour milk mixture into dry ingredients; stir just until moistened. Spoon batter into prepared pans, filling each cup about two-thirds full.

Bake in a preheated 350° oven for 10 to 14 minutes or until a toothpick inserted in center of muffin comes out clean. Cool in pans 5 minutes. Remove from pans; serve warm or cool on a wire rack.

YIELD: about 2$^{1}/_{2}$ dozen mini muffins

Mocha-Nut Muffins

Add $^{1}/_{2}$ teaspoon vanilla, $^{1}/_{3}$ cup mini chocolate chips melted, and 1 tablespoon instant coffee granules to liquid ingredients. Stir in $^{3}/_{4}$ cup mini chocolate chips and $^{1}/_{2}$ cup finely chopped toasted pecans.

YIELD: about 4 dozen mini muffins

Oatmeal Muffins

Substitute brown sugar for granulated sugar. Substitute $^{3}/_{4}$ cup quick-cooking oats for $^{3}/_{4}$ cup flour.

YIELD: about 3 dozen mini muffins

Cornmeal-Cheese Muffins

Substitute $^{3}/_{4}$ cup yellow cornmeal for $^{3}/_{4}$ cup flour. Add 1 cup finely shredded sharp Cheddar cheese.

YIELD: about 3 dozen mini muffins

Cream Cheese Muffins

Prepare muffin batter. In a small bowl, beat cream cheese, granulated sugar, and extracts until well blended. In another small bowl, combine brown sugar, flour, and cinnamon; blend in butter until mixture is crumbly. Layer the following into each muffin cup: 1 teaspoon batter, 1 teaspoon cream cheese mixture, $^{1}/_{2}$ teaspoon batter, and $^{1}/_{2}$ teaspoon brown sugar mixture. Bake following Basic Muffins recipe.

YIELD: about 4 dozen mini muffins

BASIC MUFFINS

- 1$^{3}/_{4}$ cups self-rising flour
- 3 tablespoons sugar
- $^{3}/_{4}$ cup milk
- $^{1}/_{2}$ cup butter or margarine, melted
- 2 eggs

CREAM CHEESE MUFFINS

- 1 recipe Basic Muffins
- 2 packages (3 ounces each) cream cheese, softened
- $^{2}/_{3}$ cup granulated sugar
- $^{1}/_{2}$ teaspoon lemon extract
- $^{1}/_{4}$ teaspoon vanilla extract
- $^{1}/_{4}$ cup firmly packed brown sugar
- 2$^{1}/_{2}$ tablespoons all-purpose flour
- $^{3}/_{4}$ teaspoon ground cinnamon
- 1 tablespoon butter or margarine, softened

Raspberry jam and a kiss of sweet cream cheese icing make a winning combination in these mini Oatmeal-Jam Muffins. You can count on these to disappear fast!

oatmeal-jam muffins

Line miniature muffin pans with paper baking cups; set aside.

For muffins, combine flour, brown sugar, baking powder, salt, and cinnamon in a medium bowl. Stir in oats. In a small bowl, combine milk, oil, and egg. Add milk mixture to dry ingredients; stir just until blended. Spoon 1 tablespoon of batter into each cup of prepared pans. Spoon 1/2 teaspoon of jam over batter in each cup.

Bake in a preheated 375° oven for 14 to 16 minutes or until lightly browned. Cool in pans 5 minutes. Remove from pans and cool on a wire rack.

For icing, beat cream cheese and butter in a small bowl until fluffy. Add confectioners sugar and vanilla; beat until smooth. Spoon icing into a pastry bag fitted with a large round tip. Pipe icing onto center of each muffin. Store in refrigerator.

YIELD: about 2 1/2 dozen mini muffins

MUFFINS

- 1 cup all-purpose flour
- 1/2 cup firmly packed brown sugar
- 2 teaspoons baking powder
- 1/2 teaspoon salt
- 1/4 teaspoon ground cinnamon
- 1 cup quick-cooking oats
- 1 cup milk
- 1/4 cup vegetable oil
- 1 egg, beaten
- 1/3 cup plus 1 tablespoon seedless raspberry jam

ICING

- 1 package (3 ounces) cream cheese, softened
- 3 tablespoons butter or margarine, softened
- 1 1/2 cups confectioners sugar
- 1/2 teaspoon vanilla extract

Resistance is futile! Flavored with double chocolate (cocoa and chocolate chips), this luscious treat is a cross between a muffin and bread pudding. Torn pieces of buttermilk biscuits provide the foundation.

chocolate bread pudding muffins

Line muffin pans with paper baking cups; set aside.

In a large bowl, tear biscuits into small pieces. Stir in milk; set aside to allow biscuits to absorb most of the milk.

In a medium bowl, beat eggs, butter, and vanilla until well blended. Add sugar and cocoa; beat until well blended. Stir in chocolate chips. Add chocolate mixture to biscuit mixture; stir until well blended. Let stand 5 minutes.

Spoon batter into prepared pans, filling each cup about three-fourths full.

Bake in a preheated 350° oven for 40 minutes or until a toothpick inserted in center of muffin comes out clean. Remove from pans; serve warm.

YIELD: about 18 muffins

1 can (12 ounces) refrigerated buttermilk biscuits, baked according to package directions

2 cups milk

3 eggs

3 tablespoons butter or margarine, melted

2 teaspoons vanilla extract

$3/4$ cup sugar

$1/4$ cup cocoa

1 cup (6 ounces) semisweet chocolate chips

Here's a tempting taste you don't find every day in muffins: a creamy mix of chocolate chips and peanut butter is hidden in the center of these oat bran Surprise Muffins.

surprise muffins

Line muffin pan with paper baking cups; set aside.

In a small bowl, combine peanut butter and chocolate chips; set aside.

In a medium bowl, combine flour, bran, brown sugar, baking powder, and salt. In a small bowl, whisk milk, oil, eggs, and maple extract. Make a well in center of dry ingredients and add milk mixture; stir just until moistened. Spoon about 2 tablespoons of batter into each cup of prepared pan. Spoon about 2 teaspoons of peanut butter mixture over batter in each cup. Spoon remaining batter over peanut butter mixture, filling each cup about three-fourths full.

Bake in a preheated 425° oven for 15 to 18 minutes or until tops are lightly browned. Remove from pan; serve warm or cool on a wire rack.*

YIELD: about 1 dozen muffins

***NOTE:** To reheat, cover and bake in a preheated 350° oven for 5 to 8 minutes or until heated through.

$1/2$ cup smooth peanut butter

$1/2$ cup semisweet chocolate chips

$1^1/2$ cups all-purpose flour

1 cup oat bran

$1/2$ cup firmly packed brown sugar

$2^1/2$ teaspoons baking powder

$1/4$ teaspoon salt

1 cup milk

$1/3$ cup vegetable oil

2 eggs

1 teaspoon maple extract

Not your ordinary muffins, these goodies are flavored with orange juice and chocked full of gourmet jelly beans—a yummy treat for the young or the young at heart. We baked ours in colorful silicone flower baking cups for a playful look.

jelly bean muffins

Line a muffin pan with paper baking cups;* set aside.

In a large bowl, cream butter and sugar. Add orange juice and egg; beat until blended. In a small bowl, combine flour, baking powder, baking soda, and salt. Add dry ingredients to creamed mixture; stir just until moistened. Stir in jelly beans. Spoon batter into prepared pan, filling each cup about two-thirds full.

Bake in a preheated 400° oven for 13 to 15 minutes or until a toothpick inserted in center of muffin comes out clean. Remove from pan; serve warm or cool on a wire rack.

YIELD: about 1 dozen muffins

***NOTE:** Our muffins were baked in silicone flower baking cups.

$1/3$ cup butter or margarine, softened

$1/2$ cup sugar

$2/3$ cup orange juice

1 egg

$1^1/2$ cups all-purpose flour

2 teaspoons baking powder

$1/2$ teaspoon baking soda

$1/2$ teaspoon salt

$1/2$ cup small gourmet jelly beans, coarsely chopped

These two recipes are both wonderful with hearty meals or steaming bowls of soup. Sour cream and cream-style corn make the Creamy Corn Muffins (top) extra moist. The super-loaded Sausage Cornbread Muffins are practically a meal in themselves.

creamy corn muffins

Lightly grease miniature muffin pans:* set aside.

In a medium bowl, combine cornmeal, flour, sugar, baking powder, salt, and baking soda. In a small bowl, beat corn, sour cream, butter, and egg until well blended. Add to dry ingredients; stir just until blended. Spoon batter into prepared pans, filling each cup two-thirds full.

Bake in a preheated 375° oven for 16 to 18 minutes or until tops are lightly browned and a toothpick inserted in center of muffin comes out clean. Remove from pans; serve warm.

YIELD: about 4 dozen mini muffins

*NOTE: Our muffins were baked for 18 to 20 minutes in eight 2-inch high x 2¾-inch diameter paper baking molds.

- 1 cup yellow cornmeal
- 1 cup all-purpose flour
- 2 tablespoons sugar
- 1 tablespoon baking powder
- ¾ teaspoon salt
- ½ teaspoon baking soda
- 1 can (8.5 ounces) cream-style corn
- 1 cup sour cream
- ¼ cup butter or margarine, melted
- 1 egg

sausage-cornbread muffins

Grease a 7-mold cast-iron pan (each mold is about 3-inches in diameter) or lightly grease cups in muffin pans; set aside.

In a large skillet, brown sausage over medium-high heat; drain well. In a large bowl, combine cornmeal, flour, baking powder, and salt. In a small bowl, combine sour cream, butter, eggs, and pepper sauce; beat until smooth. Fold in sausage, corn, cheese, and sweet red pepper. Spoon batter into prepared pan or muffin cups, filling each mold or cup about three-fourths full.

Bake in a preheated 375° oven for 25 to 30 minutes or until a toothpick inserted in center of muffin comes out clean. Remove from pan; serve warm or cool on a wire rack.* Store in refrigerator.

YIELD: about 14 muffins in cast-iron pan or 28 regular size muffins

*NOTE: To reheat, bake on an ungreased baking sheet in a preheated 350° oven for 8 to 10 minutes or until heated through.

- ½ pound mild pork sausage
- ¾ cup cornmeal
- ¼ cup all-purpose flour
- 1 tablespoon baking powder
- 1 teaspoon salt
- 1 cup sour cream
- ¾ cup butter or margarine, softened
- 2 eggs
- 1 teaspoon hot pepper sauce
- 1 package (10 ounces) frozen corn, thawed
- 1 cup (4 ounces) grated sharp Cheddar cheese
- ½ cup chopped sweet red pepper

BISCUITS AND MORE

Hot-from-the-oven biscuits are the ultimate comfort food! Tuck a pat of butter inside, spoon on the jam, or chock them full of nuts or cheese. Our recipes let you make them many different ways, as well as other breakfast favorites—scones, pancakes, and more.

Buttermilk and mashed sweet potatoes add richness to tender Homestyle Sweet Potato Biscuits. These are great with meals at morning, noon, or night, or you can fill them with sliced country ham for good-anytime snacks.

homestyle sweet potato biscuits

In a large bowl, combine flour, baking powder, and salt. Using a pastry blender or 2 knives, cut in butter and shortening until well blended. Add sweet potatoes and enough buttermilk to make a soft dough.

On a floured surface, lightly knead dough about 20 times. Roll out dough to ½-inch thickness. Use a 2-inch biscuit cutter to cut out biscuits. Place on an ungreased baking sheet.

Bake in a preheated 450° oven for 12 to 15 minutes or until biscuits are light golden brown. Serve warm.

YIELD: about 2 dozen biscuits

- 2 cups all-purpose flour
- 2½ teaspoons baking powder
- ½ teaspoon salt
- ¼ cup chilled butter or margarine, cut into pieces
- ¼ cup vegetable shortening
- 1 cup cooked and mashed sweet potatoes
- 5 to 7 tablespoons buttermilk

A luscious swirl of chopped pecans and brown sugar turns each of these delectable Praline Biscuits into a pretty pinwheel. Maple flavoring makes them extra yummy.

praline biscuits

In a small bowl, combine pecans, brown sugar, butter, and maple extract; set aside.

In a medium bowl, combine flour, granulated sugar, baking powder, baking soda, and salt. Using a pastry blender or 2 knives, cut shortening into dry ingredients until mixture resembles coarse meal. Add milk, stirring just until moistened.

Turn dough onto a lightly floured surface and knead about 2 minutes. Roll out dough into an 8 x 12-inch rectangle; spread pecan mixture over dough. Beginning at 1 long edge, roll up dough jellyroll style. Using a serrated knife, cut into twelve 1-inch-thick slices. Place slices, with sides touching, in a greased 7 x 11-inch baking pan.

Bake in a preheated 400° oven for 22 to 25 minutes or until lightly browned. Serve warm.

YIELD: 1 dozen biscuits

1 cup chopped pecans
1/4 cup firmly packed brown sugar
3 tablespoons butter or margarine, melted
1 teaspoon maple extract
2 cups all-purpose flour
2 teaspoons granulated sugar
1 teaspoon baking powder
1/2 teaspoon baking soda
1/4 teaspoon salt
1/2 cup vegetable shortening
3/4 cup milk

Light and airy, Angel Biscuits get their delicate taste from whipping cream and sweetened shredded coconut. You'll want to put these exquisite creations on a pedestal!

angel biscuits

In a large bowl, combine baking mix and coconut. Add cream and stir until well blended.

Turn dough onto a lightly floured surface and knead about 1 minute. Roll out dough to $1/2$-inch thickness. Use a floured 2-inch biscuit cutter to cut out biscuits. Place biscuits 2 inches apart on a greased baking sheet and brush tops with melted butter.

Bake in a preheated 400° oven for 7 to 10 minutes or until lightly browned. Serve warm.

YIELD: about $1^1/_2$ dozen biscuits

$2^1/_2$ cups buttermilk biscuit mix

$1/_2$ cup sweetened shredded coconut

1 cup whipping cream

2 tablespoons butter or margarine, melted

Cocoa, mini chocolate chips, and teensy bits of chopped pecans come together beautifully in these delicious Chocolate Biscuits. The results are classic chocolate goodness with a lightly sweet impression.

chocolate biscuits

In a large bowl, combine flour, cocoa, sugar, baking powder, salt, and cinnamon. Using a pastry blender or 2 knives, cut in butter until mixture resembles coarse meal. Stir in pecans and chocolate chips. Add milk; stir just until a soft dough forms.

On a lightly floured surface, roll out dough to $1/2$-inch thickness. Use a 2-inch biscuit cutter to cut out biscuits. Place on a greased baking sheet.

Bake in a preheated 425° oven for 10 to 15 minutes or until bottoms are lightly browned. Serve warm.

YIELD: about 2 dozen biscuits

$1^3/_4$ cups all-purpose flour

$1/_4$ cup cocoa

$1/_4$ cup sugar

1 tablespoon baking powder

$1/_2$ teaspoon salt

$1/_4$ teaspoon ground cinnamon

$1/_2$ cup butter or margarine

$2/_3$ cup finely chopped pecans

$1/_2$ cup semisweet chocolate mini chips

$2/_3$ cup milk

Whether you need just a couple or a couple dozen, easy make-ahead Freezer Biscuits are ready to pop in the oven any time you want them. But nobody says you have to wait until some other time—you can bake and serve the whole batch as soon as you get the dough prepared.

freezer biscuits

In a large bowl, combine flour, baking powder, salt, sugar, and baking soda. Using a pastry blender or 2 knives, cut sour cream and butter into dry ingredients until mixture begins to cling together. Add water, 1 teaspoonful at a time, to moisten dough; shape into a ball.

On a lightly floured surface, roll out dough to 1-inch thickness. Use a 2-inch-square biscuit cutter to cut out biscuits. Place on an ungreased baking sheet.* Cover and freeze 1 hour. Place frozen biscuits in a resealable plastic freezer bag and store in freezer.

When ready to bake, place frozen biscuits on an ungreased baking sheet. Bake in a preheated 425° oven for 15 to 17 minutes or until tops are lightly browned. Serve warm.

YIELD: about 2 dozen biscuits

***NOTE:** If you prefer not to freeze biscuits, bake in a preheated 425° oven for 10 to 12 minutes or until tops are lightly browned. Serve warm.

4	cups all-purpose flour
2	tablespoons baking powder
$1^1/_2$	teaspoons salt
1	teaspoon sugar
$^1/_2$	teaspoon baking soda
1	container (16 ounces) sour cream
$^1/_2$	cup chilled butter, cut into pieces
3	teaspoons water

Once you've tried Easy Cheddar-Garlic Biscuits, you'll make sure your pantry is always supplied with baking mix and the necessary seasonings. These flavorful delights can be made in minutes with basic ingredients and shredded sharp Cheddar cheese.

easy cheddar-garlic biscuits

In a large bowl, combine baking mix, cheese, garlic powder, and Italian seasoning. Add milk; stir until well blended.

On a lightly floured surface, roll out dough to $1/2$-inch thickness. Use a 2-inch biscuit cutter to cut out biscuits. Place on a greased baking sheet.

Bake in a preheated 425° oven for 11 to 13 minutes or until golden brown. Brush with melted butter. Serve warm.

YIELD: about 3 dozen biscuits

4 cups buttermilk biscuit mix

2 cups (8 ounces) shredded sharp Cheddar cheese

2 teaspoons garlic powder

2 teaspoons dried Italian herb seasoning

$1^1/2$ cups milk

Melted butter

You'll reel in the compliments with these golden cornmeal Hush Puppies! Minced onion and ground red pepper make them a delicious addition to a family fish fry.

hush puppies

Heat about 1^1/$_2$ inches of vegetable oil to 350° in a deep skillet.

In a large bowl, combine cornmeal, flour, onion, baking powder, sugar, salt, baking soda, and red pepper. In a medium bowl, combine buttermilk and egg; stir into dry ingredients until well blended.

Drop batter by tablespoonfuls into hot oil. Fry until golden brown and thoroughly cooked. Drain on paper towels. Serve warm.

YIELD: about 3 dozen hush puppies

Vegetable oil

1^1/$_2$ cups yellow cornmeal

^{3}/$_4$ cup all-purpose flour

3 tablespoons dried minced onion

1 teaspoon baking powder

1 teaspoon sugar

1 teaspoon salt

^{1}/$_2$ teaspoon baking soda

^{1}/$_4$ teaspoon ground red pepper

1^1/$_4$ cups buttermilk

1 egg, beaten

Made with equal parts of flour and cornmeal, these traditional Johnny Cakes are enhanced with cheese. They are so good and so fast to fix in a hot skillet that there really is no excuse for not making them!

johnny cakes

In a large bowl, combine flour, cornmeal, baking powder, salt, and baking soda. In a medium bowl, whisk together buttermilk, butter, and egg; add to dry ingredients; stir just until moistened. Fold in cheese.

In a large skillet, heat oil over medium heat. Drop tablespoonfuls of batter into hot oil. Turning once, cook 3 to 4 minutes or until brown. Place on paper towels to drain. Serve warm.

YIELD: about 1 1/2 dozen Johnny cakes

1	cup all-purpose flour
1	cup cornmeal
4	teaspoons baking powder
1	teaspoon salt
1/2	teaspoon baking soda
1 1/2	cups buttermilk
1/4	cup butter or margarine, melted
1	egg
1 1/2	cups (6 ounces) shredded sharp Cheddar cheese
1/2	cup vegetable oil

Delicious with salads and soups, Dilly Cheese Scones are fun to make in the traditional Scottish form of a mound of dough cut into triangular wedges.

dilly cheese scones

In a large bowl, combine flour, baking powder, dill weed, salt, and dry mustard. Cut in butter with a pastry blender or 2 knives until mixture resembles coarse meal. Stir in cheese. Make a well in the center of mixture; pour in milk. Mix with a fork just until blended.

With floured hands, turn out dough onto a lightly floured surface and pat into a 9-inch-diameter circle. Place on an ungreased baking sheet. Use a serrated knife to cut dough into 8 wedges (do not separate wedges). In a small cup, beat together egg and water; lightly brush over dough.

Bake in a preheated 425° oven for 12 to 15 minutes or until top is golden brown. Cut into 8 scones and serve warm.

YIELD: 8 scones

- 2 **cups all-purpose flour**
- 1 **tablespoon baking powder**
- 2 **teaspoons dried dill weed**
- 1 **teaspoon salt**
- ½ **teaspoon dry mustard**
- ¼ **cup butter or margarine**
- 1 **cup (4 ounces) shredded sharp Cheddar cheese**
- 1 **cup milk**
- 1 **egg**
- 1 **teaspoon water**

Not too moist, not too dry, but just right. That's how some people describe scones. Generous portions of blueberries and crushed pineapple ensure success for this wholesome recipe.

blueberry scones

In a medium bowl, combine ⅓ cup sugar, flour, cinnamon, baking soda, and salt; make a well in center of dry ingredients. Combine pineapple, milk, oil, and egg; add to dry ingredients. Stir just until moistened. Gently stir in blueberries. Drop heaping tablespoonfuls of batter onto a baking sheet sprayed with cooking spray. Sprinkle remaining 1 tablespoon sugar over top of batter.

Bake in a preheated 400° oven for 12 to 15 minutes or until golden brown. Serve warm.

YIELD: about 24 scones

⅓ cup plus 1 tablespoon sugar, divided

1¾ cups all-purpose flour

1 teaspoon ground cinnamon

1 teaspoon baking soda

½ teaspoon salt

1 can (8 ounces) crushed pineapple in juice, slightly drained

¼ cup skim milk

3 tablespoons vegetable oil

1 egg

1½ cups frozen blueberries, not thawed

Vegetable cooking spray

Served with a spot of tea, Peach-Almond Scones will bring a hint of international flair to an afternoon snack. Our recipe is a fruity variation of the traditional Scottish quick bread. The lightly sweet scones also lend themselves well to breakfast on the go.

peach-almond scones

In a small microwave-safe bowl, combine peaches and orange juice. Cover and microwave on high power (100%) 1 to $1^1/_2$ minutes or until juice is hot; set aside.

In a large bowl, combine flour, brown sugar, baking powder, and salt; stir until well blended. Using a pastry blender or 2 knives, cut in butter until mixture resembles coarse meal. Make a well in center of ingredients. In a small bowl, combine whipping cream, egg, and vanilla; add to flour mixture. Stir in peaches and almonds just until moistened.

On a floured surface, roll out dough to $^1/_2$-inch thickness. Use a $2^3/_4$-inch square biscuit cutter to cut out scones. Place on a greased baking sheet.

Bake in a preheated 375° oven for 10 to 12 minutes or until lightly browned and a toothpick inserted in center of scone comes out clean. Serve warm or cool on a wire rack.

YIELD: about 13 scones

1 package (6 ounces) dried peaches, finely chopped
$^1/_3$ cup orange juice
$2^1/_4$ cups all-purpose flour
$^1/_3$ cup firmly packed brown sugar
$2^1/_4$ teaspoons baking powder
$^1/_2$ teaspoon salt
$^1/_2$ cup chilled butter
$^1/_4$ cup whipping cream
1 egg
1 teaspoon vanilla extract
$^1/_2$ cup sliced almonds

Baking mix provides a head-start on Carrot-Raisin Scones. Ideal for brunch, the biscuit-like pastries feature a pleasing blend of taste sensations.

carrot-raisin scones

Combine baking mix, sugar, and orange peel in a medium bowl. Using a pastry blender or 2 knives, cut in chilled butter until mixture resembles coarse meal. Add buttermilk, raisins, and carrot, stirring with a fork just until moistened. Turn dough onto a lightly floured surface and knead 10 to 12 times. Pat dough into $1/2$-inch thickness. Use a 3-inch round biscuit cutter to cut out scones. Place 2 inches apart on a lightly greased baking sheet.

Bake in a preheated 425° oven for 10 to 12 minutes or until tops are golden brown. Brush tops of scones with melted butter. Serve warm or cool on a wire rack.

YIELD: about 1 dozen scones

2 cups buttermilk biscuit mix

1 tablespoon sugar

$3/4$ teaspoon dried orange peel

$1/2$ cup butter or margarine, chilled and cut into pieces

$3/4$ cup buttermilk

$1/2$ cup golden raisins

$1/2$ cup finely shredded carrot

2 tablespoons butter or margarine, melted

Cappuccino Waffles with Coffee Syrup are sure to provide a morning boost. The rich flavor makes an eye-opening treat.

cappuccino waffles with coffee syrup

For coffee syrup, combine coffee and sugar in a medium saucepan. Stirring constantly over medium-high heat, cook mixture until sugar dissolves. Without stirring, bring mixture to a boil; boil 2 minutes. Remove from heat; keep warm.

For cappuccino waffles, cream butter, sugar, and vanilla in a medium bowl until fluffy. In a small bowl, combine flour, dry milk, creamer, coffee granules, baking powder, salt, and cinnamon. On low speed of an electric mixer, beat dry ingredients into creamed mixture (mixture will be crumbly). Add water and eggs; stir just until blended.

For each waffle, pour about $^2/_3$ cup batter into a preheated, greased waffle iron. Bake 3 to 5 minutes or according to manufacturer's instructions. Serve warm with warm coffee syrup.

YIELD: about $1^3/_4$ cups syrup and about five 8-inch waffles

COFFEE SYRUP
- 1 cup strongly brewed coffee
- 2 cups sugar

CAPPUCCINO WAFFLES
- $^1/_2$ cup butter or margarine, softened
- 1 cup sugar
- 1 teaspoon vanilla extract
- $1^1/_3$ cups all-purpose flour
- $^1/_3$ cup nonfat dry milk
- $^1/_4$ cup non-dairy powdered creamer
- 2 tablespoons instant coffee granules
- 2 teaspoons baking powder
- $^1/_4$ teaspoon salt
- $^1/_4$ teaspoon ground cinnamon
- $^3/_4$ cup water
- 2 eggs, beaten

Your family will think you're a sweetheart for serving Chocolate Waffles, a luscious alternative to typical morning fare. Presented with a drizzling of cinnamon-spiced Marshmallow Topping, they're a unique and elegant dessert, too!

chocolate waffles with marshmallow topping

For topping, heat marshmallow creme and corn syrup over medium-low heat in a medium saucepan until marshmallow creme melts. Stir in vanilla and cinnamon; keep warm.

For waffles, cream butter and sugar in a large bowl until fluffy. Add milk, eggs, and vanilla; beat until smooth. In a small bowl, combine cake flour, baking powder, and salt. Add dry ingredients and melted chocolate to creamed mixture and blend (do not overmix).

For each waffle, pour about $1/2$ cup batter into a preheated, greased heart-shaped waffle iron. Bake 5 to 7 minutes or according to manufacturer's instructions. Serve warm with warm topping. Garnish, if desired.

YIELD: about six 7-inch waffles

MARSHMALLOW TOPPING

- 1 jar (7 ounces) marshmallow creme
- 2 tablespoons light corn syrup
- $1/2$ teaspoon clear vanilla extract
- $1/4$ teaspoon ground cinnamon

WAFFLES

- $1/2$ cup butter or margarine, softened
- 1 cup sugar
- $1/2$ cup milk
- 2 eggs
- 1 teaspoon vanilla extract
- $1^1/2$ cups sifted cake flour
- 2 teaspoons baking powder
- $1/4$ teaspoon salt
- 2 ounces semisweet baking chocolate, melted

  GARNISH: shaved semisweet baking chocolate

Enriched with oats and whole-wheat flour, Hearty Pancakes are a delicious and nutritious start to the day. The recipe makes it easy to prepare the dry mix ahead of time and store in the refrigerator.

hearty pancakes

Process oats in a food processor until coarsely ground. Add flours, buttermilk powder, sugar, baking powder, baking soda, and orange peel; process until blended. Place dry ingredients into a large bowl. Stir in raisins and almonds. Divide into 2 resealable plastic bags and store in refrigerator.

YIELD: about $6^1/_4$ cups pancake mix

To serve: Combine 1 bag pancake mix, $1^2/_3$ cups water, 1 egg, and 3 tablespoons vegetable oil in a medium bowl. Stir just until moistened.

Heat a greased griddle over medium heat. For each pancake, pour about $^1/_4$ cup batter onto griddle.* Cook until top of pancake is full of bubbles and bottom is golden brown. Turn with a spatula and cook until remaining side is golden brown. Grease griddle as necessary. Serve warm with butter and syrup.

YIELD: about 18 pancakes

*NOTE: Our pancakes were cooked in a 4-inch-wide heart-shaped pancake mold on a greased electric griddle; one recipe of batter made about 17 heart-shaped pancakes.

1	cup old-fashioned oats
2	cups all-purpose flour
$1^1/_2$	cups whole-wheat flour
1	cup dry buttermilk powder
$^1/_3$	cup sugar
3	tablespoons baking powder
1	tablespoon baking soda
1	teaspoon dried orange peel
1	cup raisins
1	cup sliced almonds, toasted
	Butter and syrup to serve

For a fresh twist on pancakes, try these Lemon-Oatmeal Pancakes. Warm Blueberry Syrup tops them off with pizzazz.

lemon-oatmeal pancakes with blueberry syrup

For blueberry syrup, combine blueberries, water, corn syrup, and pectin in a Dutch oven over medium-high heat. Stirring constantly, bring to a rolling boil. Add sugar. Stirring constantly, bring to a rolling boil again and boil 1 minute. Remove from heat. Serve warm or pour into heat-resistant jars; cover with lids and cool to room temperature. Store in refrigerator.

For pancakes, combine baking mix, milk powder, oats, sugar, and lemon zest in a large bowl. In a medium bowl, combine water and eggs; add to dry ingredients and stir just until moistened. Heat a greased griddle over medium heat.

For each pancake, pour about $1/4$ cup batter onto griddle and cook until top of pancake is full of bubbles and underside is lightly browned. Turn with a spatula and cook until remaining side is lightly browned. Grease griddle as necessary. Serve warm with butter and warm Blueberry Syrup.

YIELD: about $5^1/2$ cups syrup and 14 pancakes

BLUEBERRY SYRUP

- 1 package (12 ounces) frozen blueberries
- 2 cups water
- 1 cup light corn syrup
- 1 package ($1^3/4$ ounces) powdered fruit pectin
- 4 cups sugar

LEMON-OATMEAL PANCAKES

- 2 cups all-purpose baking mix
- $1/2$ cup nonfat milk powder
- $1/2$ cup quick-cooking oats
- 2 tablespoons sugar
- 2 teaspoons grated lemon zest
- $1^3/4$ cups water
- 2 eggs, slightly beaten
- Butter to serve

The spicy flavor of ginger, added to the rich taste of molasses in the batter, makes Gingerbread Pancakes a perfect choice for a special brunch. Don't forget the butter and syrup!

gingerbread pancakes

In a large bowl, combine flour, sugar, ginger, baking powder, baking soda, and salt. In a medium bowl, whisk buttermilk, eggs, $1/3$ cup melted butter, and molasses. Add to dry ingredients and stir just until blended.

Heat a greased griddle over medium heat. For each pancake, pour about $1/4$ cup batter onto griddle and cook until pancake is full of bubbles on top and underside is lightly browned. Turn with a spatula and cook until other side is lightly browned. Grease griddle as necessary. Transfer to a warm plate, cover with aluminum foil, and place in a 200° oven until ready to serve. Serve warm with butter and syrup.

YIELD: about $1^1/2$ dozen pancakes

$1^1/2$ cups all-purpose flour
$1/4$ cup sugar
1 teaspoon ground ginger
1 teaspoon baking powder
1 teaspoon baking soda
$1/2$ teaspoon salt
1 cup buttermilk
3 eggs, beaten
$1/3$ cup butter or margarine, melted
$1/4$ cup molasses
Butter and syrup to serve

PASTRIES

Rich and flaky or soft and crumbly, pastries are the crème de la crème of baked goods! Few can resist these spice-sprinkled rolls or tarts and turnovers filled with scrumptious fruits and creamy fillings. You'll be surprised at how easy they are to make!

Think of it as a portable piece of pie! Each of these pretty pockets is prepared with triangles cut from refrigerated pie crust and filled with amaretto-laced peaches and toasted almonds. Heart cutouts and a sprinkle of cinnamon-sugar make them extra sweet.

peach-almond pastries

Using a slotted spoon, remove peaches from pie filling (discard liquid) and place in a food processor. Add almonds, amaretto, and almond extract. Process until peaches are coarsely chopped; set aside.

Cut each pie crust into 8 triangles for a total of 16 triangles. Place 8 triangles on a baking sheet lightly sprayed with cooking spray. Spoon about 3 tablespoons of peach mixture into center of each triangle. Use a heart-shaped aspic cutter to cut hearts in centers of remaining triangles. Place cutout triangles over pie filling. Use a fork to crimp edges of dough together. Combine sugar and cinnamon in a small bowl. Lightly spray tops of pastries with cooking spray; sprinkle with sugar mixture.

Bake in a preheated 425° oven for 20 to 25 minutes or until tops are golden brown. If edges of crust brown too quickly, cover with strips of aluminum foil. Serve warm.

YIELD: 8 servings

- 1 can (21 ounces) peach pie filling
- ½ cup sliced almonds, toasted
- 2 tablespoons amaretto
- ½ teaspoon almond extract
- 1 package (15 ounces) refrigerated pie crusts, at room temperature
- Vegetable cooking spray
- 2 tablespoons sugar
- ½ teaspoon ground cinnamon

Fresh apples and cranberries make a sweet, tart filling for these easy turnovers made using frozen puff pastry sheets. Cinnamon, nutmeg, and chopped walnuts add flavor and crunch. Top them with a dusting of confectioners sugar or drizzled glaze.

cranberry-apple turnovers

For turnovers, combine apples, cranberries, sugar, walnuts, flour, cinnamon, and nutmeg in a large saucepan. Stirring occasionally, bring to a boil over medium heat. Reduce heat, cover, and simmer about 5 minutes or until apples are tender. Remove from heat.

On a lightly floured surface, cut each sheet of pastry into fourths. Place pastry squares on a greased baking sheet. Spoon about $1/4$ cup of apple mixture into center of each pastry square. Fold dough in half diagonally over filling to form a triangle; use a fork to crimp edges together.

Bake in a preheated 400° oven for 16 to 18 minutes or until golden brown.

Dust with confectioners sugar or drizzle with glaze. For glaze, combine sugar and milk in a small bowl; stir until smooth. Drizzle glaze over warm turnovers. Serve warm or at room temperature.

YIELD: 8 servings

TURNOVERS

- $2^1/2$ cups peeled, cored, and chopped tart cooking apples (about 3 apples)
- $3/4$ cup fresh cranberries
- 1 cup granulated sugar
- $1/4$ cup chopped walnuts
- 2 tablespoons all-purpose flour
- $1/2$ teaspoon ground cinnamon
- $1/4$ teaspoon ground nutmeg
- 2 sheets (one $17^1/4$-ounce package) frozen puff pastry dough, thawed according to package directions
- Confectioners sugar

GLAZE

- $1/2$ cup confectioners sugar
- 2 teaspoons milk

Perfect for nibbling with coffee or hot tea, these tiny Apricot Foldovers have a tangy filling of dried fruit inside tender cream cheese pastry. Cutting the dough with a pastry wheel creates the fluted edges.

apricot foldovers

For filling, mix all ingredients together in a medium saucepan over medium heat and bring to a boil. Cook, stirring constantly, 8 to 10 minutes or until filling thickens. Cool completely.

For pastry, combine flour and salt in a medium bowl. Using a pastry blender or 2 knives, cut butter and cream cheese into flour until mixture resembles coarse meal. Sprinkle ice water over dough, mixing quickly just until dough forms a soft ball.

On a lightly floured surface, roll out dough into a $1/4$-inch-thick rectangle. Use a pastry wheel to cut dough into 2-inch squares. Place dough on a greased baking sheet. Spoon about 1 teaspoon of filling into the center of each square. Fold dough in half diagonally over filling to form a triangle; use a fork to crimp edges together.

Bake in a preheated 350° oven for 15 to 20 minutes or until golden brown. Serve warm or cool completely on a wire rack.

YIELD: about 4 dozen foldovers

FILLING

- 1 cup chopped dried apricots
- 1 cup firmly packed brown sugar
- $1/2$ cup water
- 2 tablespoons all-purpose flour

PASTRY

- $2^1/2$ cups all-purpose flour
- $1/2$ teaspoon salt
- $3/4$ cup plus 2 tablespoons butter or margarine, chilled and cut into pieces
- 1 package (3 ounces) cream cheese, cut into pieces
- $1/3$ cup ice water

It's a good thing this recipe yields more than 4 dozen appetizers, because no one will want to stop with just one bite! Baked Onion Pastries are tasty little treats featuring a sautèed onion filling in a golden brown pastry. The fun shape is created by using a ravioli cutter to crimp circles of dough together.

baked onion pastries

For pastry, combine flour, dry mustard, salt, and red pepper in a medium bowl. Process cream cheese and butter in a food processor until blended. Add dry ingredients to creamed mixture and process just until blended. Divide dough into 4 balls and wrap in plastic wrap; chill 1 hour.

For filling, melt butter in a large skillet over medium-high heat. Add onions; cook just until onions soften. Stir in brown sugar. Continue to cook until onions are lightly browned and sugar is dissolved; remove from heat. Stir in salt, black pepper, curry powder, and red pepper.

Roll out one ball of dough into a 9-inch circle. Using a 2-inch round ravioli cutter, lightly mark circles on dough. Spoon about 1 rounded teaspoon of onion mixture into center of each circle. Roll out second ball of dough into a 9-inch circle and place on top of onion-topped dough. Use ravioli cutter to crimp edges of each pastry together. Place on a lightly greased baking sheet. Cut a small slit in tops of pastries with a knife. Repeat with remaining dough, rerolling dough scraps.

Bake in a preheated 375° oven for 15 to 20 minutes or until lightly browned. Serve warm.

YIELD: about 5 dozen appetizers

PASTRY

- 2½ cups all-purpose flour
- 1 teaspoon dry mustard
- ½ teaspoon salt
- ⅛ teaspoon ground red pepper
- 2 packages (8 ounces each) cream cheese, softened
- ¾ cup butter or margarine, softened

FILLING

- 2 tablespoons butter or margarine
- 6 cups coarsely chopped yellow onions
- 2 tablespoons firmly packed brown sugar
- ½ teaspoon salt
- ¼ teaspoon ground black pepper
- ¼ teaspoon curry powder
- ⅛ teaspoon ground red pepper

To start the day with a quick, hearty breakfast, keep a supply of Sausage Breakfast Turnovers in the freezer. The savory bites are ready to pop straight from the freezer into the oven.

sausage breakfast turnovers

In a large skillet, cook sausage over medium heat until lightly browned. Add onion and pepper; cook until vegetables are tender. Transfer sausage mixture to a colander to drain; cool.

On a lightly floured surface, roll each biscuit into a 4-inch circle. In a medium bowl, combine sausage mixture and cheese. Spoon 1 tablespoon of sausage mixture onto half of each biscuit. Leaving edges free, brush egg white on edges. Fold in half. Place biscuits on an ungreased baking sheet; press edges together with a fork. Prick tops with fork.*

Bake in a preheated 350° oven for 13 to 16 minutes or until heated through and golden brown. Serve warm.

YIELD: 30 turnovers

***NOTE:** Unbaked turnovers may be frozen for later use. Place baking sheet in freezer 1 hour or until turnovers are firm. Transfer to a resealable plastic bag; store in freezer. To bake, place frozen turnovers on an ungreased baking sheet. Let stand at room temperature 30 minutes. Bake as directed above.

1 package (16 ounces) bulk pork sausage

$1/3$ cup chopped onion

$1/3$ cup chopped green pepper

3 cans (12 ounces, 10 count each) refrigerated biscuits

1 cup (4 ounces) finely shredded Cheddar cheese

1 egg white, beaten

It's no accident that we made these little Cheese Puffs in heart shapes—everyone falls in love with them! The appetizing bites are prepared with Gruyère and Parmesan cheeses, revved up with ground white pepper and a pinch of ground red pepper.

cheese puffs

Line baking sheets with parchment paper; set aside.

In a small bowl, combine flour, salt, white pepper, and red pepper. In a heavy medium saucepan over high heat, bring milk and butter to a boil; immediately remove from heat. Add flour mixture all at once; stir with a wooden spoon until mixture forms a ball. Transfer mixture to a medium bowl. Add eggs, 1 at a time, beating well with an electric mixer after each addition. Stir in cheeses.

Spoon batter into a pastry bag fitted with a medium star tip (4B). To pipe each heart, pipe 2 dough strips into a slight "V" shape, using more pressure at top of heart and pulling down to form bottom of heart. (Heart should measure approximately $1^3/_4$ inches at widest point.) Pipe hearts 1 inch apart onto prepared baking sheets.

Bake in a preheated 400° oven for 12 to 15 minutes or until golden brown. Serve warm.

YIELD: about 6 dozen cheese puffs

$^3/_4$ cup all-purpose flour

$^1/_2$ teaspoon salt

$^1/_4$ teaspoon ground white pepper

Pinch of ground red pepper

$^3/_4$ cup milk

6 tablespoons butter

3 eggs

$^1/_2$ cup grated Gruyère cheese

$^1/_4$ cup grated Parmesan cheese

They're so rich and yummy, who would guess that both of these pastries are made from canned crescent rolls! Family members will love waking up to the aroma of buttery Chocolate Cinnamon Rolls. A sweetened cream cheese filling lends lemony flavor to the Cheese Danish Pastries.

chocolate cinnamon rolls

Unroll crescent roll dough on a lightly greased surface; firmly press dough perforations together to form a $7^1/_2$ x $14^1/_2$-inch rectangle. Spread butter over dough.

In a small bowl, combine chocolate chips, sugar, pecans, and cinnamon. Sprinkle chocolate chip mixture over buttered dough to within $1/_2$ inch of edges. Lightly press mixture into dough. Beginning at 1 long edge, roll up dough jellyroll-style. Using a serrated knife, cut into $3/_4$-inch slices. Place slices 2 inches apart on a greased baking sheet.

Bake in a preheated 375° oven for 11 to 13 minutes or until lightly browned. Serve warm.

YIELD: about 16 rolls

1 can (8 ounces) refrigerated crescent rolls
2 tablespoons butter or margarine, softened
$1/_2$ cup semisweet chocolate mini chips
2 tablespoons sugar
2 tablespoons chopped pecans
$1^1/_2$ teaspoons ground cinnamon

cheese danish pastries

In a small bowl, beat cream cheese, confectioners sugar, egg yolk, and lemon extract with an electric mixer until well blended.

Unroll crescent roll dough on a lightly greased surface; firmly press dough perforations together to form a $7^1/_2$ x $14^1/_2$-inch rectangle. Spread cream cheese mixture over dough to within $1/_2$ inch of edges. Beginning at 1 long edge, roll up dough jellyroll-style. Using a serrated knife, cut into $3/_4$-inch slices. Place slices 2 inches apart on a lightly greased baking sheet.

Bake in a preheated 375° oven for 11 to 13 minutes or until lightly browned. Serve warm.

YIELD: about 16 pastries

4 ounces cream cheese, softened
$1/_4$ cup confectioners sugar
1 egg yolk
$1/_2$ teaspoon lemon extract
1 can (8 ounces) refrigerated crescent rolls

Served warm from the oven, cinnamon-spiced Golden Monkey Bread with butterscotch-pecan glaze is a pleasing pull-apart treat. Frozen dinner rolls make this gooey creation carefree to bake.

golden monkey bread

In a small bowl, combine brown sugar and cinnamon. Tear each roll into 3 pieces. Dip each piece into melted butter and coat with brown sugar mixture. Place half of dough pieces in a greased 10-inch fluted tube pan. Sprinkle $1/4$ cup butterscotch chips and $1/4$ cup pecans over dough. Place remaining dough pieces in pan. Sprinkle remaining butterscotch chips and pecans over dough. Cover and let rise in a warm place (80° to 85°) about $2^1/2$ hours or until doubled in size.

Bake in a preheated 375° oven for 25 to 30 minutes or until golden brown. Cover with aluminum foil if bread begins to brown too quickly. Cool in pan 10 minutes. Invert bread onto a serving plate. Serve warm.

YIELD: 10 to 12 servings

1 cup firmly packed brown sugar

1 teaspoon ground cinnamon

1 package (25 ounces) frozen white dinner yeast rolls, thawed

$1/2$ cup butter or margarine, melted

$1/2$ cup butterscotch chips, divided

$1/2$ cup chopped pecans, divided

Made with canned biscuits and a buttery brown sugar topping, Quickie Cinnamon Rolls are simple to prepare a day or two ahead and store in the refrigerator, ready to bake as soon as hungry loved ones rise for the day.

quickie cinnamon rolls

In a small saucepan over medium heat, stir brown sugar, butter, and cinnamon until butter melts. Pour butter mixture into a 9-inch pie plate. Sprinkle pecans over butter mixture. Dip one side of each biscuit in mixture; place coated side up in pan.

Bake in a preheated 400° oven for 12 to 18 minutes or until bread is lightly browned. Serve immediately.

YIELD: 10 cinnamon rolls

$3/4$ cup firmly packed brown sugar

$1/4$ cup butter or margarine

1 teaspoon ground cinnamon

$1/4$ cup chopped pecans

1 can (10 biscuits) refrigerated large biscuits

So hungry you could eat a whole pie? Try one of these Easy Pecan Tarts instead.
With whipped cream on top, they offer big satisfaction!

easy pecan tarts

Combine eggs, pecans, brown sugar, butter, vanilla, and salt. Spoon pecan mixture into tart shells. Place filled shells on a baking sheet.

Bake in a preheated 425° oven for 16 to 18 minutes or until filling is set. Cool completely on a wire rack. Garnish, if desired.

YIELD: 8 tarts

2 eggs, lightly beaten

1 cup chopped pecans, reserving 1 tablespoon for garnish, if desired

$3/4$ cup firmly packed brown sugar

2 tablespoons butter or margarine, melted

1 teaspoon vanilla extract

$1/8$ teaspoon salt

8 frozen unbaked 2-inch-diameter tart shells, thawed

GARNISHES: whipped cream, reserved chopped pecans

These Miniature Fruit Tarts are a luscious way to celebrate the bounty of nature! Topped with colorful fruit and berries, a rich white chocolate cream filling is nestled in flaky pastry shells.

miniature fruit tarts

For pastry, combine sugar and salt in a bowl. Cut in butter with a pastry blender or 2 knives until almost blended. Combine egg yolks and water in a small bowl; stir into butter mixture. Add flour, mixing just until blended. Divide dough in half and wrap in plastic wrap. Refrigerate 1 hour.

Working with half of the dough at a time, press about 1 tablespoon of dough into each small tart pan. Prick bottoms and sides of dough with a fork. Place on baking sheets and bake in a preheated 350° oven for 20 to 25 minutes or until lightly browned. Cool completely before removing pastry shells from pans.

For filling, melt white chocolate chips with cream in a double boiler over medium heat, stirring until smooth. Remove from heat and beat in cream cheese. Spoon filling into cooled pastry shells. Arrange assorted fruits on top.

For glaze, melt jelly and sugar in a small saucepan over low heat; cool slightly. Brush gently over fruits. Chill several hours before serving.

YIELD: about 18 tarts

PASTRY

- $1/2$ cup confectioners sugar
- $1/4$ teaspoon salt
- $1/2$ cup butter, cut into pieces and softened
- 2 egg yolks, beaten
- 3 tablespoons cold water
- 2 cups all-purpose flour

FILLING

- $3/4$ cup white chocolate chips
- 3 tablespoons whipping cream
- 4 ounces cream cheese, softened

  Assorted fresh fruits: blueberries, strawberries, mandarin oranges, grapes, blackberries, and kiwis

GLAZE

- $2/3$ cup apple jelly
- 2 teaspoons sugar

With their sunny look and zesty flavor, Lemon Curd Tarts are always a popular choice. Pop one in your mouth for a taste of happiness!

lemon curd tarts

For crust, combine flour, sugar, and salt in a mixing bowl. Using a pastry blender or 2 knives, cut butter into flour until mixture resembles coarse meal. Sprinkle ice water over dough, mixing quickly just until dough forms a soft ball. Wrap dough in plastic wrap and refrigerate 1 hour.

On a lightly floured surface, use a floured rolling pin to roll out dough to $1/8$-inch thickness. Cut dough into circles about $1/4$-inch larger than tart pans. Press dough into pans. Prick bottoms and sides of dough with a fork. Crimp edges with fork. Refrigerate 30 minutes.

Place tart pans on a baking sheet and bake in a preheated 400° oven for 13 to 15 minutes or until very lightly browned. Cool completely before removing pastry shells from pans.

For lemon curd, combine all ingredients in a heavy non-aluminum saucepan over medium-low heat. Cook, stirring constantly, until butter melts and mixture thickens slightly. Do not allow mixture to boil. Remove from heat. Transfer mixture to a bowl to cool. Cover and refrigerate at least 2 hours before serving.

To serve, spoon lemon curd into pastry shells.

YIELD: about 16 tarts

CRUST
- $1^1/4$ cups all-purpose flour
- 2 tablespoons sugar
- $1/4$ teaspoon salt
- $1/2$ cup butter, chilled and cut into pieces
- 3 tablespoons ice water

LEMON CURD
- 6 egg yolks
- 1 cup sugar
- $1/2$ cup fresh lemon juice
- 6 tablespoons butter, cut into pieces
- $1^1/2$ tablespoons grated lemon zest
- $1/8$ teaspoon salt

These flaky tarts, with their creamy plum filling, are perfect for sweet little celebrations. Use colorful paper liners in your miniature muffin tins to give the tarts a party look.

sugarplum tarts

Line miniature muffin pans with paper baking cups; grease cups. Set pans aside.

For crust, cream butter and sugar in a large bowl until fluffy. Add egg yolks, 1 at a time, beating well after each addition. Add remaining ingredients; stir until a soft dough forms. Press about $1^1/_2$ teaspoons dough into bottoms and up sides of each paper cup.

For filling, spoon about $^1/_2$ teaspoon of jam into each cup; set aside. In a large bowl, combine sugar, flour, and salt in a large bowl. Add whipping cream, half and half, and vanilla. Using highest speed of an electric mixer, beat cream mixture until thick and fluffy, about 4 to 5 minutes. Spoon about 1 tablespoon of cream mixture into each cup.

Bake in a preheated 350° oven for 30 to 35 minutes or until filling is set in center and crust is brown. Cool in pans 10 minutes. Remove from pans; serve warm or cool on a wire rack.

YIELD: about 5 dozen tarts

CRUST

- $^3/_4$ cup butter or margarine, softened
- $^1/_2$ cup sugar
- 2 egg yolks
- $1^3/_4$ cups all-purpose flour
- $^1/_8$ teaspoon salt
- $^3/_4$ teaspoon vanilla extract

FILLING

- 1 jar (10 ounces) red plum jam
- 1 cup sugar
- $^1/_4$ cup all-purpose flour
- $^1/_8$ teaspoon salt
- 1 cup whipping cream
- $^1/_2$ cup half and half
- 2 teaspoons vanilla extract

Cream cheese pastry surrounds a spoonful of raspberry jam and chopped almonds in each of these flavorful tarts. Keep some in the freezer for a quick snack whenever you're craving a special treat.

raspberry-almond tarts

In a mixing bowl, beat butter and cream cheese until creamy. Add flour and beat until blended. Cover and chill one hour.

Shape pastry into 24 one-inch balls. Press balls into bottom and up sides of each ungreased cup of a miniature muffin pan. Spoon 1/2 teaspoon of raspberry jam into each cup. Stir together sugar, almond paste, and egg; spoon 1 teaspoon of sugar mixture over jam and sprinkle with chopped almonds.

Bake in a preheated 325° oven for 30 to 35 minutes. Cool slightly in pan on a wire rack; remove from pan and cool completely. Freeze up to one month, if desired.

YIELD: 2 dozen tarts

- 1/2 cup butter or margarine, softened
- 1 package (3 ounces) cream cheese, softened
- 1 cup all-purpose flour
- 1/3 cup seedless raspberry jam
- 1/2 cup sugar
- 1/3 cup almond paste, crumbled
- 1 egg
- 1/2 cup whole blanched almonds, coarsely chopped

Macadamia Nut Tarts feature luscious caramel-coated nuts heaped in a pastry shell. Dried lemon peel perks up the tender crust.

macadamia nut tarts

For crust, cream butter, sugar, and lemon peel in a large bowl until fluffy. In a medium bowl, combine flour, cornstarch, and salt. Stir dry ingredients into creamed mixture, mixing just until dough is crumbly. On a lightly floured surface, roll out dough to $1/4$-inch thickness. Use a 3-inch biscuit cutter to cut out dough. Transfer dough to greased $2^1/2$-inch-diameter tart pans. Prick dough with a fork. Place tart pans on a baking sheet.

Bake in a preheated 350° oven for 16 to 18 minutes or until lightly browned. Cool in pans 10 minutes; remove from pans and cool completely on a wire rack.

For topping, combine butter, brown sugar, and honey in a medium saucepan. Stir constantly over medium-high heat until mixture comes to a boil. Boil 1 minute, without stirring, until mixture thickens and large bubbles begin to form. Remove from heat; stir in nuts and cream. Spoon about 2 tablespoons of mixture into each tart crust. Cool completely.

YIELD: about 20 tarts

CRUST

- $1^1/2$ cups butter or margarine, softened
- $2/3$ cup sugar
- $2^1/2$ teaspoons grated dried lemon peel
- 3 cups all-purpose flour
- $1/2$ cup cornstarch
- $1/2$ teaspoon salt

TOPPING

- $1/2$ cup plus 2 tablespoons butter or margarine
- $1/2$ cup firmly packed brown sugar
- $1/3$ cup honey
- 3 cups macadamia nuts
- $2^1/2$ tablespoons whipping cream

Cashew-Fudge Tarts are brownie-like treats nestled in flaky pastry. Coffee flavor enhances the rich bites.

cashew-fudge tarts

For pastry, combine flour and sugar in a medium bowl. Using a pastry blender or 2 knives, cut butter into dry ingredients until mixture resembles coarse meal. Knead until a soft dough forms. Shape 1/2 tablespoon of dough into balls. Press balls of dough into bottoms and up sides of each greased cup of a miniature muffin pan.

For filling, whisk sweetened condensed milk and egg in a medium bowl. In a small bowl, combine water and coffee; stir until coffee dissolves. Add coffee mixture, chocolate chips, flour, vanilla, and baking powder to milk mixture; beat with an electric mixer until smooth. Stir in 1 cup cashews. Spoon about 1 tablespoon of filling into each cup. Sprinkle remaining 1/2 cup cashews evenly over filling in each cup.

Bake in a preheated 350° oven for 25 to 30 minutes or until set in center. Cool in pans 10 minutes. Remove from pans and cool completely on wire racks.

YIELD: about 5 1/2 dozen tarts

PASTRY

- 3 cups all-purpose flour
- 6 tablespoons sugar
- 1 1/2 cups butter or margarine, softened

FILLING

- 1 can (14 ounces) sweetened condensed milk
- 1 egg
- 1 tablespoon hot water
- 1 teaspoon instant coffee granules
- 1 package (6 ounces) semisweet chocolate chips, melted
- 2 tablespoons all-purpose flour
- 1 teaspoon vanilla extract
- 1/4 teaspoon baking powder
- 1 1/2 cups lightly salted dry-roasted cashews, coarsely chopped and divided

A favorite Tex-Mex dessert, these traditional pastries are best served hot. Because of the way they puff up like little pillows, you can tear off a corner and fill the airy center with honey.

sopaipillas

In a large bowl, combine flour, baking powder, and salt. Using a pastry blender or 2 knives, cut in shortening. Make a well in center of flour mixture and add scalded milk. Mix until a soft dough forms.

On a lightly floured surface, knead dough about 15 times or until smooth and elastic; set aside 10 minutes. Use a lightly floured rolling pin to roll out dough to $1/8$-inch thickness. Use a sharp knife to cut into 3-inch squares.

Fill a large Dutch oven with about 2 inches of oil. Heat oil to 365°. Place 3 or 4 sopaipillas at a time in pan; cook until lightly browned and puffed, turning once. Transfer to paper towels to drain. Serve immediately by tearing an opening in each sopaipilla and pouring honey inside.

YIELD: about $2^1/2$ dozen sopaipillas

4 cups all-purpose flour
1 teaspoon baking powder
1 teaspoon salt
1 tablespoon shortening
$1^1/2$ cups scalded milk, cooled to room temperature
Vegetable oil
Honey to serve

Real kid-pleasers, these scrumptious Cinnamon-Sugar Pretzels are easy to make using frozen white bread dough. Just roll the dough into ropes and follow our knotting diagrams. Don't keep all the fun to yourself—let the kids help!

cinnamon-sugar pretzels

On a lightly floured surface, use a floured rolling pin to roll out each loaf to a 6 x 12-inch rectangle. Cut each rectangle of dough into twelve 1 x 6-inch strips. Shape each strip into a 14-inch-long roll. Refer to Fig. 1 and shape each roll into a pretzel shape.

Fig. 1

2 loaves (one 32-ounce package) frozen white bread dough, thawed according to package directions

Vegetable cooking spray

1 cup sugar

1 teaspoon ground cinnamon

Place pretzels 1 inch apart on a baking sheet sprayed with cooking spray. Spray tops of pretzels with cooking spray, cover, and let rise in a warm place (80° to 85°) 1 hour or until doubled in size.

In a medium bowl, combine sugar and cinnamon; set aside.

Bake in a preheated 350° oven for 18 to 20 minutes or until lightly browned. Lightly spray both sides of pretzels with cooking spray. Place pretzels, 1 at a time, in sugar mixture and spoon sugar over until well coated. Serve warm.

YIELD: 2 dozen pretzels

KITCHEN TIPS

*NOTE: For additional tips, see Success With Breads on page 7.

MEASURING INGREDIENTS

Liquid measuring cups have a rim above the measuring line to keep liquid ingredients from spilling. Nested measuring cups are used to measure dry ingredients, butter, shortening, and peanut butter. Measuring spoons are used for measuring both dry and liquid ingredients.

To measure flour or granulated sugar: Spoon ingredient into nested measuring cup and level off with a knife. Do not pack down with spoon.

To measure confectioners sugar: Sift sugar, spoon lightly into nested measuring cup, and level off with a knife.

To measure brown sugar: Pack sugar into nested measuring cup and level off with a knife. Sugar should hold its shape when removed from cup.

To measure butter, shortening, or peanut butter: Pack ingredient firmly into nested measuring cup and level off with a knife.

To measure liquids: Use a liquid measuring cup placed on a flat surface. Pour ingredient into cup and check measuring line at eye level.

To measure honey or syrup: For a more accurate measurement, lightly spray measuring cup or spoon with cooking spray before measuring so the liquid will release easily from cup or spoon.

SOFTENING BUTTER OR MARGARINE

To soften butter, remove wrapper from butter and place on a microwave-safe plate. Microwave 1 stick 20 to 30 seconds at medium-low power (30%).

SOFTENING CREAM CHEESE

To soften cream cheese, remove wrapper from cream cheese and place on a microwave-safe plate. Microwave 1 to $1^1/_2$ minutes at medium power (50%) for an 8-ounce package or 30 to 45 seconds for a 3-ounce package.

WHIPPING CREAM

For greatest volume, chill a glass bowl, beaters, and cream until well chilled before whipping. In warm weather, place chilled bowl over ice while whipping cream.

TOASTING NUTS

Nuts will stay crisp better and have fuller flavor if toasted before combining with other ingredients. To toast nuts, spread nuts on an ungreased baking sheet. Stirring occasionally, bake 8 to 10 minutes in a preheated 350° oven until nuts are slightly darker in color. Watch carefully to prevent overcooking.

PREPARING CITRUS FRUIT ZEST

To remove outer portion of peel (colored part) from citrus fruits, use a fine grater or fruit zester, being careful not to cut into the bitter white portion. Zest is also referred to as grated peel.

BEATING EGG WHITES

For greatest volume, beat egg whites at room temperature in a clean, dry metal or glass bowl.

BUTTER

Recipes were tested using salted butter, unless otherwise specified in recipe. When softening butter in the microwave, be careful not to let it melt, as melted butter results in flatter baked goods. If margarine is used, use one labeled "margarine" instead of "spread." Corn oil margarines will make a softer dough, which will increase chilling time.

MAKING CHOCOLATE CURLS

Making chocolate curls for garnishes is not difficult, but it does take a little practice. The chocolate should be the correct firmness to form the curls, neither too soft nor too hard. Different types of baking chocolates may be used, but the most common ones are semisweet and unsweetened. They are usually packaged in boxes containing 1-ounce squares. There are several methods for making chocolate curls.

To make small, short curls, hold a baking chocolate square in your hand for a few minutes to slightly soften chocolate. Rub chocolate over shredding side (large holes) of a grater to form curls.

For medium-size curls, use a vegetable peeler or chocolate curler (available in kitchen specialty stores) to shave the wide side (for wide curls) or thin side (for thin curls) of a chocolate square.

To make long, thin, loosely formed curls, melt 6 chocolate squares and pour into a foil-lined $3\frac{1}{4}$ x $5\frac{1}{4}$-inch loaf pan. Chill until chocolate is set (about 2 hours). Remove from pan and remove foil. Rub chocolate over shredding side (large holes) of a grater to form curls.

To make large curls, melt about 5 chocolate squares and pour into a jellyroll pan or onto a cookie sheet. Spread chocolate over pan. Chill about 10 minutes. Scrape across surface of chocolate with a long metal spatula, knife, teaspoon, or chocolate curler to form curls. The spatula and knife will form long, thin curls and the teaspoon and curler will form shorter curls. Return pan to refrigerator if chocolate becomes too soft. Use a toothpick to pick up curls.

GIFT PRESENTATION IDEAS

To enhance your food gift, try some of the following ideas for pretty presentations.

DISHES

Check flea markets, thrift shops, or your own cabinets for one-of-a-kind trays, plates, or other dishes. A piece of vintage china will make your homemade goodies especially irresistible. Also, inexpensive tins and platters can be found at discount or hobby stores. A sheet of clear or colored cellophane adds a professional finish!

BAGS

Gift bags are handy ways to dress up food gifts. There are hundreds of beautiful gift bags in all sizes and shapes available at stores everywhere, or you can dress up plain bags. Be creative!

JARS

Some breads can be baked in canning jars for convenient gift-giving. Just be sure that the recipient knows the bread must be eaten while fresh, because it has not been processed properly for food preservation. To dress up the jar, simply place a pretty cloth over the lid and gather it with a rubber band or a length of ribbon.

GIFT TAGS

No matter what container or theme you choose, don't forget to make a special gift tag. You can use rubber stamps, scraps of fabric and paper, craft foam, and motifs cut from old greeting cards. Scrapbooking supplies are especially nice to use. The possibilities are endless!

BASKETS

So easy to tote anywhere, baskets are handy for delivering food gifts. Just line the basket with colorful tissue or a square of cloth and place your wrapped or packaged food inside.

metric equivalents

The recipes that appear in this cookbook use the standard United States method for measuring liquid and dry or solid ingredients (teaspoons, tablespoons, and cups). The information on this chart is provided to help cooks outside the U.S. successfully use these recipes. All equivalents are approximate.

METRIC EQUIVALENTS FOR DIFFERENT TYPES OF INGREDIENTS

A standard cup measure of a dry or solid ingredient will vary in weight depending on the type of ingredient. A standard cup of liquid is the same volume for any type of liquid. Use the following chart when converting standard cup measures to grams (weight) or milliliters (volume).

Standard Cup	Fine Powder (ex. flour)	Grain (ex. rice)	Granular (ex. sugar)	Liquid Solids (ex. butter)	Liquid (ex. milk)
1	140 g	150 g	190 g	200 g	240 ml
¾	105 g	113 g	143 g	150 g	180 ml
⅔	93 g	100 g	125 g	133 g	160 ml
½	70 g	75 g	95 g	100 g	120 ml
⅓	47 g	50 g	63 g	67 g	80 ml
¼	35 g	38 g	48 g	50 g	60 ml
⅛	18 g	19 g	24 g	25 g	30 ml

USEFUL EQUIVALENTS FOR LIQUID INGREDIENTS BY VOLUME

¼ tsp					=	1 ml	
½ tsp					=	2 ml	
1 tsp					=	5 ml	
3 tsp	=	1 tbls		½ fl oz	=	15 ml	
		2 tbls	=	⅛ cup	=	1 fl oz	=	30 ml
		4 tbls	=	¼ cup	=	2 fl oz	=	60 ml
		5 ⅓ tbls	=	⅓ cup	=	3 fl oz	=	80 ml
		8 tbls	=	½ cup	=	4 fl oz	=	120 ml
		10 ⅔ tbls	=	⅔ cup	=	5 fl oz	=	160 ml
		12 tbls	=	¾ cup	=	6 fl oz	=	180 ml
		16 tbls	=	1 cup	=	8 fl oz	=	240 ml
		1 pt	=	2 cups	=	16 fl oz	=	480 ml
		1 qt	=	4 cups	=	32 fl oz	=	960 ml
					=	33 fl oz	=	1000 ml	=	1 liter

USEFUL EQUIVALENTS FOR DRY INGREDIENTS BY WEIGHT

(To convert ounces to grams, multiply the number of ounces by 30.)

1 oz	=	1⁄16 lb	=	30 g
4 oz	=	¼ lb	=	120 g
8 oz	=	½ lb	=	240 g
12 oz	=	¾ lb	=	360 g
16 oz	=	1 lb	=	480 g

USEFUL EQUIVALENTS FOR LENGTH

(To convert inches to centimeters, multiply the number of inches by 2.5.)

1 in					=	2.5 cm		
6 in	=	½ ft			=	15 cm		
12 in	=	1 ft			=	30 cm		
36 in	=	3 ft	=	1 yd	=	90 cm		
40 in					=	100 cm	=	1 m

USEFUL EQUIVALENTS FOR COOKING/OVEN TEMPERATURES

	Fahrenheit	Celsius	Gas Mark
Freeze Water	32° F	0° C	
Room Temperature	68° F	20° C	
Boil Water	212° F	100° C	
Bake	325° F	160° C	3
	350° F	180° C	4
	375° F	190° C	5
	400° F	200° C	6
	425° F	220° C	7
	450° F	230° C	8
Broil			Grill

recipe index